ISBN 978-1-60091-677-9

Book design by: Perel Leah Levitin

Distributed by:
Israel Bookshop Publications
501 Prospect Street
Lakewood, NJ 08701

Tel: (732) 901-3009
Fax: (732) 901-4012
www.israelbookshoppublications.com
info@israelbookshoppublications.com

Printed in Bulgaria

Distributed in Israel by:
Tfutza Publications
P.O.B. 50036
Beitar Illit 90500
972-2-650-9400

Distributed in Australia by:
Gold's Book and Gift Company
3-13 William Street
Balaclava 3183
613-9527-8775

Distributed in Europe by:
Lehmanns
Unit E Viking Industrial Park
Rolling Mill Road,
Jarrow, Tyne & Wear NE32 3DP
44-191-430-0333

Distributed in South Africa by:
Kollel Bookshop
Northfield Centre
17 Northfield Avenue
Glenhazel 2192
27-11-440-6679

Dedication

לעילוי נשמת אבי מורי

החבר אריה בן ר׳ משולם ז״ל

LEO HEXTER

A quiet, dignified, refined person with an aristocratic carriage – a noble spirit, a Jew who stood tall. He always smiled and was easy to get along with.

At age nineteen he just barely escaped, by himself, from Nazi Germany, arriving penniless in America. He struggled to immediately support himself in a six-day work-week economy and was uncompromising on שמירת השבת.

He, together with his אשת חיל Martha Hexter שתבדל לחיים טובים וארוכים, invested boundless time, effort and resources in their children, and was ever thankful to הקב״ה for the returns. He was so very proud of his children, his grandchildren and his great-grandchildren and very much appreciated, and was grateful for, the זכות he had to see them all follow בדרך התורה ומצוות.

He saw great importance in, and devoted significant time to, community institutions, Khal Adas Jeshurun, Yeshiva Rabbi Samson Raphael Hirsch and Agudas Yisroel.

He was always קובע עתים לתורה, and constantly conveyed its importance to his children and grandchildren. A strong believer in Rav Hirsch's תורה עם דרך ארץ, he worked at it throughout his life. He taught the primacy of תורה while showing how it fit with דרך ארץ.

תהא נשמתו צרורה בצרור החיים

יהי זכרו ברוך

Dedication

IN LOVING MEMORY OF OUR BELOVED FATHER

הרב אליהו מאיר בן הרב דוד ז״ל
RABBI ELIYAHU MEIR WEINBERGER

Our father grew up in the community of the Schiff Shul in Vienna, Austria, and was orphaned at a young age during the Holocaust. He was spared when he was sent to England on the Kindertransport, which took him to Cardiff, South Wales and later Gateshead, England. There, his *rebbi*, Rav Nachman Dovid Landynski, and other *gedolei Yisrael* had a profound influence early on in his youth. Throughout his life he would relate to his children and grandchildren the beauty and grandeur of this period in his life.

After he immigrated to the United States, he married our dear mother תבלח״ט and built an illustrious Torah family. He dedicated his life to teaching תינוקות של בית רבן for over fifty years, beginning in the Gateshead Boarding School and then at Yeshiva Toras Emes Kaminetz in Brooklyn.

Throughout his life he was connected to great Torah luminaries such as the Klausenberger Rebbe, Bobover Rebbe and the Bluzhever Rebbe. He heard *shiurim* from Rabbi Yitzchak Piekarski זצ״ל and Rabbi Zelig Epstein זצ״ל, always treasuring these precious opportunities. He carried his unique *mesorah* of the ideological views of the חתם סופר dynasty with great pride.

He lived a life of *chessed*, as he would seek out people in the hospital or at home who needed a visit, and was instrumental in starting the Bikur Cholim in Jamaica, Queens. Above all, his sterling character, integrity and his total devotion to our dear mother and his family are some of the outstanding virtues for which he will be remembered by all who knew him.

יהי זכרו ברוך

Dedication

IN LOVING MEMORY OF OUR DEAR PARENTS

הוחבר מריה יעקב אליעזר בן הוחבר נפתלי

בריינע בת ור׳ צבי הלוי

LOU AND LOTTIE HERRMANN

After escaping the horrors of Nazi Germany and arriving on the shores of the United States, our parents, Lou and Lottie Herrmann, met and married. As immigrants to a new land and culture, they came into contact with individuals who were not always committed to שמירת המצוות. As a result, the early years of their marriage with young children were characterized by a more secular lifestyle.

One of their favorite activities was to take walks through Fort Tryon Park in the Washington Heights area of Upper Manhattan to enjoy the beautiful vistas and flowers. On one of these occasions, they were introduced to Mr. Leo Hexter, who was waiting for his wife to give birth in the hospital across the street. This introduction represented the beginning of a special relationship that would impact the rest of their lives.

Both Leo ז״ל and Martha תבלח״ט Hexter befriended our parents with unconditional love and acceptance, an uncommon phenomenon in the *frum* world of that time where the inclusion of those less religiously committed was not the norm. Our parents exchanged regular Shabbos meal invitations and Pesach Sedarim as well. The Hexter children treated us as their siblings. Leo and our father eventually became *chavrusos* and learned הלכה למעשה together for many years.

We feel honored to share in the dedication of this *sefer* and extend heartfelt *hakaras hatov* to Rabbi Naftoli Hexter and his dear wife Helen, for both creating and publishing these *divrei Torah*.

Our gratitude to your dear parents and to each of you – Charlie, Herbie, Paulette and Judy – is manifest in the families we have been *zocheh* to raise.

יהי זכרם ברוך

RONNIE AND JENNIFER HERRMANN & FAMILY

CARRIE AND RONNY WACHTEL & FAMILY

BATSHEVA AND RAPHAEL GREENBAUM & FAMILY

The Children & Grandchildren of Kenny Herrmann ז״ל

URI MAYERFELD
250 BATHURST GLEN DRIVE
THORNHILL, ON
CANADA L4J 8A7

הרב אורי שרגא מאירפלד
ראש הישיבה
ישיבת נר ישראל
טארנטא, קנדה

לעילוי נשמת

הרב חיים נפתלי אברהם בן ר׳ שמואל הלוי ויהודית בת ר׳ דוד

מורי וחמי הרב נפתלי פרידלר זצ"ל שנולד בגרמניה זכה לידבק בימי גידולו להרב הצדיק רבי משה שניידר זצ"ל. כל ימיו היה קורא אותו "דער רבי". וכנראה רבות הושפע הרב נפתלי מה"ברען" (האש) של רבו זצ"ל. כשהעביר הרב שניידר את ישיבתו מפרנקפורט ללונדון, אנגליה, הבחור ר׳ נפתלי נסע עמו (ובכן ניצל מחורבן השואה).

בסוף המלחמה ארגן הרב אליהו דסלר זצ"ל, כולל בעיר גייטסהייד, בצפון אנגליה, מטובי הלמדנים שנמלטו, מאירופא החרבה, ונטפל ר׳ נפתלי (בעוד בחור) לכולל. בכולל קראו לר׳ נפתלי ה"קאכלעפעל" (רוח חיים) של החבורה ונתדבק להרב דסלר ולדרכו הסלולה במוסר ובמחשבה.

אחר תקופה קצרה הר׳ נפתלי נשא הרבנית יהודית ז"ל שגם היא היתה מפליטי גרמניה ובערה בלבה רצון עז לינשא לתלמיד חכם.

לסבות משפחתיות ובהסכמת וברכת רב דסלר נסעו הרב ורבנית פרידלר לשכונת "וואשינגטאון הייטס" בנוא יארק ושם התחילה תקופה של הרבצת התורה וזיכוי הרבים. הרב נפתלי היה לו עין חדה להכיר אפילו במי שהיה נראה בעל הבית רצון אמיתי ללמוד תורה. וסביבו נצטברה חבורה חשובה. כל ערב למדו אתם גמרא בעיון והוא הדריך אותם ללמוד בסברא ישרה ובהבנה נכונה.

הרב יוסף ברויער זצ"ל הקים קהילה לצורך פליטי גרמניה על יסודות של "תורה עם דרך ארץ" על פי קבלתו מהרב שמשון רפאל הירש זצ"ל. מיד הכיר שהרב פרידלר מחונן בכשרון מיוחד לחנך הדור החדש (אחר החורבן). כךה נעשה קשר מיוחד בין הרב ברויער והרב פרידלר של הערצה ואהבה הדדית. אף על פי שהרב ברויער דבק במסורה של "תורה עם דרך ארץ", והרב פרידלר קבל מרבותיו תורה לשם תורה, הצד השוה שבהם היה –לימוד התורה. והמשיכו יחד לבנות הישיבה ע"ש רש"ר הירש. בתקופה מאוחרת נעשה ראש הישיבה של ישיבת נר ישראל בטארנטא, קנדה ושם הרביץ תורה והמשיך להעמיד תלמידים. בתקופה אחרונה עבר למאנסי וגם שם יסד כוללים והרביץ תורה לרבים. ועד היום טובי הלמדנים זוכרים ידיעתו המקפת וסברותיו העמוקות בש"ס ופוסקים.

אהבתו ללמוד תורה ומוסר עשה רושם לכל מי שזכה לראותו, ויחד עם אהבתו לכל יהודי עד שכל מי שנשא ונתן עמו הושפע גם לאהבת למוד תורה. הרב פרידלר ז"ל היה לו כח הסברה נפלאה ותבע מתלמידיו דקדוק בסברא ישרה וידיעה ברורה בכל סוגיא.

המחבר של הספר הזה הרב נפתלי הכסטר שליט"א זכה לקרבה מיוחדת וגם לרבות אשתו שתחי׳ כמו שפרט בדבריו.

בתור אחד מבני המשפחה של הרב פרידלר זצ"ל אנו מכירים טוב להמחבר ובני משפחתו שהחליטו לעשות מזכרת לזכרון של עטרת ראשנו זצ"ל.

בברכת תודה וידידות

אורי שרגא מאירפלד
טארנטא, ניסן תשע"ט

הרב אהרן פלדמן

RABBI AHARON FELDMAN
421 YESHIVA LANE, APT. 3A, BALTIMORE, MD 21208
TEL.: 410-6539433 FAX: 410-6534694
STUDY: 410-4847200 EXT. 6050; DIRECT LINE: 443-5486050
E-MAIL: RAF@NIRC.EDU

ROSH HAYESHIVA

NER ISRAEL RABBINICAL COLLEGE

ראש הישיבה

ישיבת נר ישראל

בס"ד צום הרביעי תשע"ח

July 1, 2018

HASKAMA

Rabbi Naftali Hexter, a well-known Baltimore Principal, has composed a unique book.

It is based on new insights into the weekly Parasha, each demonstrated by inspiring stories. These are accompanied by pithy, original aphorisms summarizing the insights, presented in a background of unusually attractive graphics. The messages are inspiring and the aphorisms and graphics make forgetting them very difficult.

I am sure the public will enjoy and benefit greatly from this book.

With respect,

Rabbi Aharon Feldman

RABBI MOSHE HEINEMANN
6109 Gist Avenue
Baltimore, MD 21215
Tel. (410) 358-9828
Fax. (410) 358-9838

משה היינעמאן
אב"ד קייק אגודת ישראל
באלטימאר
טל. 7778-764 (410)
פקס 8878-764 (410)

בס"ד

הנה ידידי הרב החשוב מאוד נעלה הרב נפתלי הכטער שליט"א הגיש לפני ספרו
היחיד במינו אשר בשם אמרי שפר יקרא, וכשמו כן הוא, מסודר לפי פרשיות
התורה ולפי המועדים שמתם שאב דרכיה של ישרות, של אמונה, ובטחון, מהלכים
של חסד, הכרת טובה והנהגות טובות. כל אלה ע"פ תורתנו הקדושה עם מעצים
מן החיים היום יומיים ועשו רושם של אמונה ושל דביקות בהקב"ה עלי ועל אחרים
כל זה מעיד על רום מעלתו של הרב המחבר ועל טוהר נשמתו. אמרתי לעצמי שזה
החיבור מצוה לפרסמו ברבים כדי שיהנו ממנו כל עם ישראל. הוא דבר השוה לכל
בין לאנשים ובין לנשים בין לבוגרים ובין לתלמידים בין לזקנים ובין לנערים בין
לבני תורה ובין למקיימי מצות בין למאמינים ובין לעדיין בלתי מאמינים – הנמצא כזה
ספר השוה לכל נפש.

יזכהו הקב"ה עם אשתו וכל הנלוים אליו שיזכה להאריך להפיץ תורת השיתב"ש
בבריות גופא ונהורא מעליא ויתפרק וישתזב מן כל עקא ומכל מרעין בישין, מרן
די בשמיא יהא בסעדוהי כל זמן ועידן.

ועל כ"ז באתי עה"ק לכבוד המחבר בשטי בשבת לסדר וירא א-לקים כי טוב ששה
ועשרים יום לחדש תשרי שנת חמשת אלפים ושבע מאות ושבעים ותשע לבריאת עולם
משה בהה"ר ברוך גד-כל-יה כ"ל מספחת היינעמאן החונ"פ יתא באלטימאר

Table of Contents

PREFACE 11

ACKNOWLEDGMENTS 13

INTRODUCTION 15

בראשית TEFILLAH 16

נח THE MIRACLE OF NATURE 18

לך לך BITACHON: THE ANTIDOTE TO WORRY 20

וירא THE ART OF GIVING 22

חיי שרה DRESSING SMART 24

תולדות LOOKING BEYOND 26

ויצא DO YOU "LOVE" FISH? 28

וישלח AN ETERNAL PEOPLE 30

וישב DO WE STAND BY OUR PRINCIPLES? 32

מקץ HOW MEANINGFUL ARE OUR DREAMS? 34

ויגש THE DARKNESS OF GALUS 36

ויחי HUMILITY AS A DRIVING FORCE 38

שמות WHEN IT'S GOOD TO BE PICKED ON 40

וארא BECOMING GREAT 42

בא WHEN QUANTITY DOES COUNT 44

בשלח/שבת שירה IMPROVING THE QUALITY OF A MITZVAH 46

יתרו ONE SYMPHONY 48

משפטים REFINED JUSTICE 50

תרומה RECIPE FOR LIFE 52

תצוה WISDOM 54

כי תשא THE SIGN OF SHABBOS 56

ויקהל ELEVATED WISDOM 58

פקודי BEING FAITHFULLY HONEST 60

ויקרא REAL FREEDOM 62

צו EXPRESSING THANKS 64

שמיני THE MAIN THING 66

תזריע WINDOWS AND MIRRORS 68

מצורע FINDING THE LIGHT IN THE TUNNEL 70

אחרי מות/יום כיפור JUST BE HUMBLE 72

קדושים A DIVINE STANDARD 74

אמור A PRICELESS GIFT 76

בהר	TORAS HASHEM	78
בחוקתי	HOLDING ON TO THE SPARK	80
במדבר/שבועות	EVERYONE COUNTS	82
נשא	FOR THE SAKE OF HARMONY	84
בהעלתך	CHANGE?!	86
שלח	FINDING KEDUSHAH	88
קרח	THE QUAKING OF ENVY	90
חקת	LIVING A DOUBLE STANDARD	92
בלק	JUST TAKE THE FIRST STEP	94
פנחס	TRUE SHALOM	96
מטות	CONFUSING PRIORITIES	98
מסעי	THE MASTER PLAN	100
דברים/שבת חזון	HASHEM'S UNCONDITIONAL LOVE	102
ואתחנן/שבת נחמו	ON BEING CONTENT	104
עקב	HASHEM'S HIDDEN HAND	106
ראה	READ - WHAT YOU SEE!	108
שופטים	FAITH IN OUR CHACHAMIM	110
כי תצא	TRUSTING IN HASHEM	112
כי תבוא	GRATITUDE	114
נצבים	STANDING TOGETHER	116
וילך	OUR YELLOW LIGHT	118
האזינו	SCALING THE SKIES	120
וזאת הברכה	IT'S ALL GOOD	122
ראש השנה	PASSING LIFE'S TESTS	124
סוכות	TEMPORARY OR PERMANENT?	126
פסח/שירת הים	SENSITIVITY	128

Preface

This *sefer* is a tribute to four families whose lives impacted each other immensely. Over the years and extending over two continents, Hashem "wove the threads" of these four families together, creating a most magnificent tapestry, exposing unbelievable השגחת ה'. The heads of these *mishpachos* were spared from the European cauldron and came to this country not knowing what the future had in store for them. Their story is our story! We must appreciate the רחמי שמים as we see how the Hand of Hashem sowed the seeds of their bright future during the darkest of times.

הזורעים בדמעה ברנה יקצרו (תהלים קכו, ה) – *Those who tearfully sow, will reap with glad song.*

My late father, Mr. Leo (Aryeh) Hexter ז"ל, and להבל"ח my mother, may she be *bentched* with good health and אריכת ימים, provided me with guidance and the "space" which I needed while growing up. For this I am forever grateful. My father was a businessman who was קובע עתים לתורה, gave *shiurim* on Shabbos, and was responsible for bringing generations of Yidden תחת כנפי השכינה. He greeted everyone with a smile and endeared himself to all. The steps that led up to his arrival in America from Germany in November 1938 are detailed in the story of

פרשת לך לך in this *sefer*. He personified the ideals of Rabbi Samson Raphael Hirsch as he lived a life of תורה עם דרך ארץ.

My mother, Mrs. Martha Hexter עמו"ש, arrived here from Germany in September 1939, after the war had broken out. She was just seventeen years old, all alone, not knowing a word of English. She left her parents, brother and sister behind, in the hope that she would earn enough money in America to help bring her family to safety. Sadly, when she had the money, it was too late. This *sefer* is in her honor.

My parents married in December 1942, not knowing the fate of their parents. Shortly afterwards they found out that all of their immediate family members (except for my father's brother, who escaped to England) were among the six million *kedoshim* who were killed על קדוש ה' – ה' ינקום דמם.

My late father-in-law, Rabbi Erwin (Eliyahu Meir) Weinberger ז"ל, was raised in Vienna, Austria. His life was saved thanks to the Kindertransport in 1938, which took him to England (see the details in פרשת ויקרא in this *sefer*). In Gateshead, England, he was influenced by Rav Dessler זצ"ל and was a "בן בית" of Rav Dovid Dryan זצ"ל

and Rabbi and Mrs. Friedler זצ"ל. His relationship with the Friedlers was renewed when he came to America and ultimately resulted in the *shidduch* between my wife and me. In 1947, he came to New York and was an elementary school *rebbi* in Yeshivas Toras Emes in Boro Park, as well as in Talmud Torah for about fifty years. He saw the unique potential in each child and was מקרב Yidden in his adult education classes, even before it was in vogue. Thanks to his warm and non-judgmental attitude toward everybody, many people today attribute their religious commitment to him.

My mother-in-law, Mrs. Debora Weinberger-Blumenberg עמו"ש, was born in Zurich and lived there while war was raging all around her. She vividly remembers how her parents hosted people whose lives were spared by crossing over into Switzerland. After the war, she came to America to visit her close relatives who escaped from Germany, and in 1948, she married my father-in-law. She thanks the Ribono Shel Olam that the lives of her parents and siblings were spared during those dark days of the Holocaust. This *sefer* is in her honor.

When looking back at our family's history we stand in awe of our parents. They had no parents here to assist them and they were alone. With an eye toward the future and with a deep sense of *emunah* and *bitachon*, they began to rebuild that which was lost.

מה גדלו מעשיך ה' מאד עמקו מחשבותיך (תהלים צב, ו) – *How great are Your deeds, Hashem, exceedingly profound are Your thoughts.*

This *sefer* is also a tribute to my *rebbi*, Rav Naftoli Friedler זצ"ל. He was not only my *rebbi* and *rosh yeshivah* in the Beis Midrash of Yeshiva Rabbi Samson Raphael Hirsch, but also our *shadchan*. He was determined yet understanding, and filled with *ahavas haTorah* and a love for his *talmidim*. He was warm and friendly and frequently sought out for his *da'as Torah*. Since my in-laws and the Friedlers were close friends, and their home was always open, my wife spent much time there. Rabbi

Friedler fled *kavod*, although it pursued him even after his passing (see the story of פרשת אחרי מות in this *sefer*). He always made himself available to me and to my wife to discuss whatever concerns we may have had. May he and his *rebbetzin* be מליצי יושר for our family and for all his descendants.

כל המקיים נפש אחת מישראל מעלה עליו הכתוב כאילו קיים עולם מלא (סנהדרין לז) – *He who sustains one Jewish life is considered by the Torah as if he has sustained the entire world.*

The "entire world" in our context may very well be the Herrmann family. My father befriended Mr. Lou and Lottie Herrmann ז"ל (see the story of פרשת במדבר in this *sefer*) early on in their married life and inspired them to live a religious lifestyle. Growing up, the Herrmanns and the Hexters were, for all practical purposes, one unit. We lived near each other, we grew up together and we spent our summer vacations together. It was a truly mutualistic relationship from which we all grew. The "seeds" planted through this relationship have borne fruit for three generations (and counting בעזהשי"ת).

May the Torah learned in this *sefer* be a *zechus* for the *neshamos* of these four families שהלכו לעולמם...

Mr. Leo Hexter
החבר אריה בן משולם

Rabbi Eliyahu Meir Weinberger
ר' אליהו מאיר בן הרב דוד

Rabbi and Mrs. Naftoli Friedler
ר' חיים נפתלי אברהם בן ר' שמואל הלוי
ויהודית בת ר' דוד

Mr. and Mrs. Lou Herrmann
החבר אריה יעקב אליעזר בן החבר נפתלי
ובריינע בת ר' צבי הלוי

Acknowledgments

I am grateful to all those who have extended themselves so that this *sefer* could be produced in a most magnificent and beautiful way.

I thank my older brother, **Dr. Charles Hexter and his wife Aviva**, of Rechovot, Israel, for their assistance. He painstakingly researched our family's lineage and even visited *kivrei avos* in Germany. This gave us all a deeper appreciation of the miracle of our survival and the incredible proliferation of our respective families after the Holocaust. We will never forget my sister-in-law, Ellen Hexter ה"ע (nee Sondhelm), for her שמחת החיים, kindness and generosity. She left an indelible impression upon all of us.

A deep debt of gratitude is due to my sister **Paulette and her husband Dr. Martin Katzenstein**, staunch supporters of the Riverdale Orthodox community. Marty always has time to lend a listening ear or generously give medical advice to anyone, whether it be inside or outside of the family.

My brother-in-law **Mr. Samson Bechhofer and his wife Judy** (my sister) are likewise pillars of the Washington Heights community. Samson, being the grandson of Rabbi Dr. Joseph Breuer זצ"ל, tirelessly perpetuates the dream of his illustrious grandfather, in deed and in thought. I, along with many others, thank him for the legal advice which he dispenses generously.

My brother-in-law **Rabbi Dovid Weinberger and his wife Adina** have given me encouragement and offered some very insightful comments in the publication of this work. He is a published author and a *talmid chacham* in his own right, who has given sage counsel to a large number of people. We always enjoy the opportunity of spending time with their wonderful family.

I greatly value the relationship that I enjoy with my brother-in-law **Rabbi Moshe Frank and his wife Esti** of Ellenville, New York. Our stimulating discussions have helped shape my way of thinking as I frequently tap into Moshe's erudition on a wide range of topics. Their open home in the mountains has provided a Shabbos respite for many of those in need.

Hakaras hatov is extended to the **children of Rabbi and Mrs. Friedler** ז"ל. Our relationship is that of family. We frequently reminisce about our youthful days together, especially those summers spent in Hunter, New York. Upon hearing of our literary project, they were enthusiastic to contribute to this effort.

I am humbled by the generosity of **Dr. Ronnie and Mrs. Jennifer Herrmann** of Monsey, New York, and of **Mrs. Carrie (Herrmann) and her husband Dr. Ronny Wachtel** of Yerushalayim. Their partnership in this work represents a deep, continuing bond which began between our parents years ago.

יְשַׁלֵּם ה' פָּעֳלֵךְ וּתְהִי מַשְׂכֻּרְתֵּךְ שְׁלֵמָה מֵעִם ה' אֱלֹקֵי יִשְׂרָאֵל (רות ב, יב) –
May Hashem compensate you for your work and may a full reward be given to you.

Thanks are also extended to **Mrs. Shani Rosenbaum**, Bais Yaakov Middle School secretary, and **Mrs. Chaya Statman**, librarian, for typing and proofreading much of the original and current document.

The staff at Israel Bookshop Publications have worked tirelessly to ensure the production of an attractive work of high quality. My debt of gratitude to them knows no bounds.

The original work had no artwork. Unbeknownst to me, my wife forwarded it to **Mrs. Perel Leah Levitin**, a very talented graphic artist, who added her creative artistic talent. The pictures add a dimension to my lessons that I never dreamt possible and made the aphorisms come alive. I owe a deep debt of gratitude to her.

The lion's share of appreciation goes to my partner in life, **Helen** 'שתחי, whose constant encouragement helped bring this work to light. May Hashem *bentch* my עזר כנגדו with good health so that she may continue to be the remarkable example of kindness and wisdom and together may we be *zocheh* to enjoy our growing family, עד מאה ועשרים שנה.

Naftoli Hexter
ב' ניסן תשע"ט

Introduction

הפך בה והפך בה דכולא בה (אבות ה, כו)

Delve into it and continue to delve into it for everything is in it.

The Torah is not only Hashem's prescription for how a Jew is to live his life, but also how a Jew is to think throughout his life. What is the attitude with which we should approach the various challenges that constantly confront us day in and day out?

The lessons contained in this *sefer* address all of the above. As we go through the weekly *parshah* we distill Hashem's messages so that the reader clearly sees each practical application. The message is then "packed" into a lucid aphorism, making it easy to remember and readily available to apply to a "real life" situation.

This work is based upon classes that I have been *zocheh* to teach over many years at the Rabbi Benjamin Steinberg Bais Yaakov Middle School in Baltimore, Maryland. As I saw my students grow through these aphorisms, I decided to make these *shiurim* available to the public. I received many positive comments from parents who discussed these lessons around their Shabbos table, and found the original stories interesting and inspiring.

The original composition was a family effort and together with my older children, we carefully reviewed each paragraph, judging its clarity, accuracy and relevance. I deeply value their input, coming from a young yet scholarly perspective. May Hashem continue to shower His blessings upon all my children and their families as they are a continuous source of *nachas* to my wife and myself.

ויהי נעם ה' אלוקינו עלינו ומעשה ידינו כוננה עלינו
ומעשה ידינו כוננהו (תהלים צ, יז)

May the pleasure of Hashem remain our lot, let the work of our hands be established upon us, and may You establish the work of our hands.

פרשת בראשית
Tefillah

וכל שיח השדה טרם יהיה בארץ וכל עשב השדה טרם יצמח כי לא המטיר ה'
אלקים על הארץ ואדם אין לעבד את האדמה. (ב, ה)

Now all trees of the field were not yet on earth and all the grass of the field had not yet sprouted, for Hashem had not sent rain upon the earth and there was no man to work the soil. (2:5)

Rashi explains how the end of the *pasuk*, *and there was no man to work the soil*, connects to its beginning: When Hashem created the vegetation on the third day it was not accompanied by rain. The grass just came to the surface of the ground but did not flourish. Three days later, when Adam Harishon was created, he realized that rain was needed so he instinctively *davened* to Hashem. Only then did the rain begin to fall and only then did the plants and trees begin to grow. Hashem waited for Adam to appear on earth so that he could appreciate the benefits of rain. And he was only able to access this *brachah* once he *davened* for it. We learn from this that Hashem may withhold His gifts (rain, children, good health, livelihood, *shidduchim*, etc.) in order to motivate us to *daven* and not to take His kindness for granted.

In addition, Hashem desires a relationship with Man. This is why our Matriarchs, Sarah, Rivkah and Rochel, were all barren by nature and could only conceive once they *davened*.

Hashem incorporated *tefillah* into the process of creation to teach us the centrality of prayer in building a loving relationship with Him as we sow the seeds of gratitude at the same time.

Can you recall an episode that prompted you to *daven* better?

Rabbi and Mrs. Yaakov Hirsch* had a child who was not well from birth. They would take him to the hospital for regular visits, as well as for emergencies. The regular doctors and nurses were thoroughly familiar with his case and had been extraordinarily supportive of him.

On December 25th in the early hours of the evening, their dear son, Avraham Dov ה"ע, had an attack. Suddenly, his stomach became bloated. Obviously, something was very wrong. They rushed him to the hospital, where due to the holiday, the "regulars" were not on duty. In the Emergency Room, the doctors assessed the situation. His heartbeat was faint and his blood pressure dangerously low. He needed surgery to see what was going on inside, but the doctors feared that due to Avraham Dov's physical instability, he would die in transport to the operating room. The doctor told Rabbi and Mrs. Hirsch, "There is nothing we can do to save him." The Hirsches told the doctors, "You do what you have to do, and we'll do what we have to do." Rabbi Hirsch then proceeded to call the local *kollel* to ask that Avraham Dov ben Rochel Devora be included in everyone's *tefillos* for Maariv. Rabbi and Mrs. Hirsch then went into their own corners and cried to Hashem to spare the life of their child. Less than an hour later the doctors came out, saying in amazement, "We don't know what happened, but his vital signs have stabilized and we can now take him into the O.R."

When recalling this episode, Rabbi Hirsch says that it is in moments like these that Hashem is saying, "I don't need long *tefillos*, just talk to Me."

* All names have been changed

Hashem likes us near, He wants us to call; **THAT'S WHY WE DON'T HAVE EVERYTHING, AFTER ALL.**

קרוב ה' לכל קוראיו לכל אשר יקראהו באמת (תהלים קמה, ח)

The Miracle of Nature

The Torah gives us an exact timeline of when particular events of the *mabul* (flood) occurred. Since we know that there are no extra words in the Torah, what is the significance behind this information? What message is Hashem trying to convey to us through this extraordinary detail?

Rabbi Samson Raphael Hirsch explains that the "*mabul* schedule" intimates that these events were not haphazard. Without these details it would be possible for someone to read the events of this great deluge as a catastrophic natural phenomenon. It would be perceived as a major historical event in which the world was inundated by a random, unprecedented global flood. To read the events of the *mabul* in such a way would be nothing short of distorting reality.

The generation of the *mabul* were lawless, amoral people whose selfishness and cruelty shook the foundation on which man was created. Hashem took deliberate and prescribed action to punish His creation so that mankind would understand what Hashem's priorities are.

עולם חסד יבנה – *The world is built on kindness.* It cannot be sustained through man's selfish lust for pleasure. The Torah delineates the exact timeline of the flood's progress so that no one can claim that this inundation was simply a fluke of nature. The Designer carefully orchestrated this event with total precision according to His prescribed schedule. The *mabul* was clearly Hashem's retribution on a civilization that robbed the world of the Creator's design for humanity.

Hashem hides His miraculous world behind a veil called "nature." According to Rabbi Samson Raphael Hirsch, this is alluded to in the word עולם (world), which is derived from the word נעלם (hidden). It is our responsibility not only to lift this veil but also to praise Hashem for His awesome creations. Do we comprehend that the sun is precisely 93 million miles away from our planet? If we were any closer, we would incinerate; if we were any further, we would freeze. Can we begin to fathom the human brain which contains 30 billion nerve cells with 10 trillion connections? What "accident" is responsible for the eye's retina, with millions of tiny nerve cells that can distinguish between dim light, bright light and colors? We cannot allow man's egocentrism to hijack the truth. We cannot subscribe to a culture's hidden agenda to deny Hashem credit for His creation, let alone fail to recognize Him as the Master Designer of our universe.

> **What natural phenomena help you connect to Hashem?**

Years ago, my mother and I spent a day in the Bronx Botanical Gardens where many magnificent and exotic plants are cultivated and grown. Although we were surrounded by the world's most exquisite creations, the Divine Designer was not given an ounce of credit. Every plaque describing a plant's biology used terms which disguised the True Architect. Words such as "evolved," "naturally developed" or "equipped naturally" were consistently used to camouflage G-d's handiwork.

As our children were growing up in California, we would take trips to the most magnificent natural sights, where we would try to capture Hashem's majesty. When we passed lofty mountains, sparkling streams or striking flora and fauna, we would exclaim to our children, "Look at that Magma." This, we explained, was an acrostic of "*Mah Gadlu Maasecha Hashem*" (How great are Your deeds, Hashem).

However, even one's noblest efforts can backfire. After we moved to Baltimore, we took an overnight trip to western Maryland where the mountains and lakes were simply breathtaking. In our desire to show our children the sun's precision we checked the local papers for the exact time of sunrise so that we could *daven Shemoneh Esrei K'vasikin* – as soon as the sun rose above the eastern horizon. We arose early, traveled to a designated spot and began to *daven*. Right before *Shemoneh Esrei*, we paused in silence, anticipating sunrise in the direction we were facing. We waited and waited, but no sun appeared. Imagine our shock when twenty minutes later we turned our heads to see "the star of the show" shining from another direction. We all chuckled and turned to *daven Shemoneh Esrei* toward the "new east," as proven by the sun's arrival.

Perhaps the greatest tragedy resulting from science's commandeering of "nature" from its legitimate Author is the diminution of man to a mere animal. When we visited the Cheyenne Mountain Zoo in Colorado Springs, we noticed a sign alongside the gorillas which read: "We're so similar – how can we not care?"

Nature is not natural;
IT'S SUPERNATURAL, NATURALLY.

מה גדלו מעשיך ה' מאד עמקו מחשבותיך (תהלים צב, ו)

Bitachon: The Antidote to Worry

Hashem directs Avram to travel to the Land of Canaan because in Canaan he and his family will have *brachah*. Trusting in Hashem explicitly, Avram takes Sarai his wife and Lot his nephew to Canaan, but there is a famine in that land. Avram does not challenge Hashem's directive but decides to move his family down to Mitzrayim (Egypt). Rashi maintains that Avram passed this test by not questioning Hashem, despite the fact that he was now forced to leave the land to which Hashem had told him to go.

Ramban contends that Avram "sinned a great sin" and should not have left Canaan. He should have had *bitachon* (trust) that Hashem would continue to support him despite the famine. Avram, continues the Ramban, had no right to expose his wife to the dangers of Mitzrayim.

Bitachon – trust in Hashem is a major quality that a Jew is expected to possess. Trust, explains Rav Shimon Schwab זצ"ל, is a product of *emunah* – faith in Hashem. It is that mitzvah which says that after all of one's most valiant efforts (*hishtadlus*), one knows that ultimately, whatever happens is for the best since it comes from a Loving Father in Heaven.

The Hebrew word for "worry" is דאגה. When we examine that word we see that it contains the first letters of the *Aleph-Beis* – skipping *beis*. That *beis* stands for *bitachon*. Since *bitachon* cannot coexist with דאגה, there is no *beis* in it. Worrying is produced when we lack total trust in Hashem.

The story is told of a Jew who walked around with his arms extended above his head the whole day. No one could convince him to lower his arms. Finally, someone took him to the rebbe for a possible solution to this bizarre situation. The rebbe stood next to the simpleton and mimicked him by extending his own arms above his own head. Turning to the fool the rebbe said, "Okay, you can now lower your arms." Amazingly, the fool complied. The rebbe explained that this person thought that he was holding up the whole world and was frightened to lower his arms lest "the world tumble." When he was assured that someone else would "hold up the world," he lowered his arms.

Although this story sounds absurd, many of us imitate the fool figuratively, thinking that we are "holding up our world." Too many of us think that only our own efforts will determine our future. This attitude leads to anxiety and worry. If we can learn and internalize the message of *bitachon*, our lives would be happier and less stressful.

What are your worries and how could *bitachon* eliminate or minimize them?

A year after Hitler ימ"ש came to power in Germany, my paternal grandfather, Mr. Gustav Höchster הי"ד*, saw "the handwriting on the wall." In 1934, he came home from a local business trip and told his family, "They killed a Jew right in front of me. There is no future for the Jews here in Germany." Although he himself would not abandon his aging father, he immediately took steps to secure a visa to America for his fifteen-year-old son, Leo (my father).

My grandfather remembered that a great-uncle of his had visited from America in 1902. This great-uncle had a grandson in Cleveland, (whom we will call) Mr. Robert Green. Would this relative of means agree to supply an affidavit of support for my father? Without this document, the United States government would not consider an application for a visa. My grandfather directed my father to be honest in his request for an affidavit from Mr. Green with one major stipulation. He must state that he could only work six days a week but not on Shabbos. Mr. Green quickly replied that in no way would he agree to such an arrangement. It was just five years after the Great Depression with ten million Americans still unemployed. How could any individual make such an outrageous request? Although my father must have felt crushed, my grandfather הי"ד said, "Don't worry, something good will come of it." I can only imagine the degree of disappointment and apprehension that my father must have felt, especially in light of the mounting anti-Semitism in Germany. Yet my grandfather's level of *bitachon* supported his forthright attitude and determination not to compromise on *shemiras Shabbos*.

Continuing with his *hishtadlus*, my grandfather contacted a cousin in New York, Mr. Shenkolevsky. Mr. Shenkolevsky also contacted Mr. Green in Cleveland to allay his fears about the integrity of my father and to assure him that he would never need to actually support him. Mr. Green now acquiesced and provided the necessary affidavit.

Although it took years for the application to be processed, my father arrived safely on these shores on November 3, 1938, about a week before Kristallnacht. Without a high level of *bitachon*, my grandfather would never have had the drive to support all the efforts that were taken to secure my father's safety.

*My father followed his father's request to change the family name upon his arrival in America.

Today is the tomorrow

YOU WORRIED ABOUT YESTERDAY.

23

ברוך הגבר אשר יבטח בה' והיה ה' מבטחו (ירמיהו יז, ז)

פרשת וירא
The Art of Giving

In the first eight *pesukim* of the *parshah*, Avraham demonstrates the quintessential manner of extending kindness. We find him at the age of ninety-nine, just three days after his *bris milah*, "at the entrance of his tent," waiting for guests. Rashi explains that initially, Hashem discouraged the presence of travelers by creating an intense heat so that Avraham could recuperate. When He saw Avraham's disappointment, He had these "travelers" appear. When Avraham sees the travelers (actually angels), he rushes to greet them and convinces them to stay. He explains to them that it is no imposition since he'll just give them a little bit to eat, and then they can continue on their way. Once they agree to stay, Avraham storms into action in an effort to complete the mitzvah of *hachnasas orchim*. He enlists the help of his wife, Sarah, and seizes the opportunity to train his son, Yishmael, in the mitzvah of hosting guests. After all the preparations have been completed, an elaborate meal is placed in front of the travelers while Avraham remains standing, ready to help in any way.

The *Torah Hakedoshah* vividly captures the enthusiasm and eagerness of Avraham to perform *chessed*. Avraham is clearly not just going through the motions of being hospitable; he is truly caring and sincere. He doesn't ask, for example, "Can I offer you something?" but rather he presents them with fresh food and earnestly anticipates that they will partake of it. It is no wonder that *Chazal* learn from this episode that our deeds are to exceed our speech – אמור מעט ועשה הרבה.

We therefore refer in *Shemoneh Esrei* to the Love of Kindness – אהבת חסד. The Chafetz Chaim writes that this is telling us the attitude that a person must possess when extending kindness. One can easily see if a person is doing *chessed* "mechanically" or if it is being done out of a love to give. Doing *chessed* happily doesn't just enhance the mitzvah – it defines it.

> How can you improve your attitude toward the great mitzvah of *chessed*?

It was in the fall of 2006, when my father-in-law, Rabbi Eliyahu Meir Weinberger זצ"ל, was admitted to Lenox Hill Hospital in Manhattan for triple bypass surgery. There were some tense moments, but *baruch Hashem*, the outcome was very successful. My wife, sister-in-law and mother-in-law were with him for Shabbos when they had an opportunity to meet some very special people.

It is no small challenge to feel the *kedushah*, warmth and serenity of Shabbos in a hospital room. So when a spirited Mr. Mendy Greenberger entered the room Friday night with rugelach and assorted pareve chocolates in hand, he was joyfully welcomed. The chocolates even had a personalized message on them, reading, "*Gut Shabbos, Refuah Shelaimah*." He added as well a sparkle of Shabbos to the room by covering the patient's bed tray with a beautiful white tablecloth. Wishing to infuse some *simchah* and inspiration into the sterile white walls of the hospital, he proceeded to sing the most beautiful *zemiros*. After he finished singing, he realized that there were some pressing needs that had not been attended to. He left the room quietly, returning a few minutes later with a pillow, blanket and *negel vasser*.

Who was this "*malach Hashem*" who was sent from Above? It became known to our family that the Greenbergers are members of the Lenox Hill Bikur Cholim who visit patients every Shabbos. They do not sit down for their own Friday night Shabbos *seudah* until late in the evening, after they have made their "rounds" in the hospital.

On Shabbos day both Mr. and Mrs. Greenberger came to engage the family in a lively conversation and to make sure that all of their material and spiritual needs were met. The signature style of Avraham Avinu in the performance of *chessed* is being perpetuated by the Greenbergers and by everyone else who extend themselves with sincerity, warmth and love.

Chessed
requires going
that extra mile,
WHILE STILL
WEARING
YOUR SPECIAL
SMILE.

רודף צדקה וחסד ימצא חיים צדקה וכבוד (משלי כא, כא)

Dressing Smart

Eliezer, the trusted servant of Avraham, is returning to Eretz Yisrael having fulfilled his mission. Riding on the camel that he is leading is Rivkah Imeinu, the wife-to-be of Yitzchak Avinu. The Torah tells us that as Yitzchak comes in view of Rivkah she takes her veil and covers her face, as an obvious expression of modesty and humility.

The hallmark of the Jewish woman is found in the way she carries herself as an *ishah tzenuah* (a modest woman). Dovid Hamelech in Tehillim states (*Tehillim* 12:144), *Our daughters are like cornerstones crafted in the form of a palace.* Rav Shimon Schwab ל"זצ (Selected Essays, page 52) writes that the "palace" referred to here is the Beis Hamikdash. The Jewish woman can become a living Beis Hamikdash; "This is the *kedushah* of Jewish womanhood." Her potential is enormous. The Torah's attitude toward a woman's dress and demeanor belies the Torah's respect for the true essence of the Jewish woman. There is nothing more important for the future of Klal Yisrael than to produce intelligent mothers who patiently raise children and inspire them through love, compassion and sensitivity. A woman's true worth is undermined when the clothing she wears is designed to attract the attention of others. Rather than to enhance her appearance, it cheapens it. This is why Dovid Hamelech says:

כל כבודה בת מלך פנימה – *All the honor of a king's daughter is inward.*

The priority that a Jewish woman must place on the mitzvah of *tznius* is encapsulated by Rav Schwab when he writes (Ibid, page 91), "While He has commanded men, for instance, to wear *tzitzis* and *tefillin*, He has given the same mandate to women through the laws of *tznius*, modesty of Jewish clothing."

Today, unfortunately, the multi-billion-dollar fashion industry has become a "fishing" industry. Fashion designers produce provocative styles and throw them out on the proverbial "fishing line" to see who will bite. They trap their bewildered customers without a care as to what message the wearer will be sending. Today, being a "smart" consumer includes "dressing smart" and not allowing the fashion moguls to cheapen our true worth.

What arguments would you make against the attitude of the fashion designers?

When Rav Shimon Schwab ל"זצ wanted to explain the concept of *tznius* to us he used the analogy of a *kallah's* wedding ring. On the one hand, no *chassan* would think of presenting his *kallah* with a diamond ring packaged in a brown paper bag. This blatantly would undermine the value of its content. So too, we need to care for and dress our body appropriately since it contains the most beautiful and unique *neshamah*. On the other hand, he would say, imagine a *kallah* who is presented a most expensive diamond ring and savors only the gorgeous velvet box. The *kallah*, instead of valuing the precious content, stares at the exterior and admires the box with such enthusiasm that the special ring inside is relegated to trivia. So too, the Jewish woman must be careful to follow the *halachos* of *tznius* so that her personality, her inner worth, is primary and the exterior is secondary.

Tragically, the Jewish people have been targeted for persecution more than any other people. Our enemies never seem to be content with the degree of savagery that they can commit against our people. The story is told of one town in which the Jewish girls were ordered to line up to be tortured and humiliated in a most inhumane way. The girls would then have their hair knotted to a horse's tail. At a galloping speed the horse was to drag its helpless victim through the streets of the city. One righteous girl asked for a few moments to prepare herself. She ingeniously secured her dress below her knees with pins so that she would not have to compromise her modesty, perhaps during the last moments of her life.

מי כעמך ישראל – *Who is like Your people, Yisrael!*

כל כבודה בת מלך פנימה (תהלים מה, יד)

Looking Beyond

Eisav returns from hunting in the field, and the Torah tells us that he is exhausted. He sees his twin brother, Yaakov, simmering a red soup which he is preparing to give to his father, Yitzchak, as a meal of condolence. Yitzchak had just become an *avel* (mourner) upon the death of his father, Avraham. *Chazal* tell us that Avraham's death was hastened to spare him the pain of seeing his grandson, Eisav, go astray. Eisav then proceeds to ask Yaakov to give him some of that "very red stuff." The *pasuk* continues to inform us that since he asked for that "very red stuff," he was therefore called Edom (meaning "red"). How can we understand that this name was given to him simply because he called the food "red"?

The Seforno explains that when Eisav identified this soup only by its appearance and not by its content, he was revealing something about his personality. Eisav was a superficial person who did not look beyond that which he initially saw. He was so removed from civility, due to his preoccupation with hunting and killing, that he referred to his food only by its appearance. He came home, worn out and tired – he saw the red soup and demanded to have that red "stuff." He didn't even notice what it really was – he just saw red. Thus, the Torah informs us that he was called Edom since through his choice of words, he displayed his "true colors."

The Gemara in *Chagigah* (12b) quotes Rav Yossi as saying, *"Woe to those people who see but don't realize what they are seeing."* Hashem expects His people to be introspective: to look beyond appearances and to be able to identify things and events for what they truly are.

What do you see but give little thought to?

As a Jew goes through life, the Hand of Hashem is often transparent to the untrained eye. Identifying significant happenings and appreciating and realizing their Divine source is often challenging, yet very important. *Hashgachah pratis* (individual Divine supervision) is frequently veiled by seemingly unconnected events, and we often need to "connect the dots" and look beyond the moment.

It was May 24, 2004, Erev Shavuos, and I needed some material at Home Depot. Rather than going myself, I invited my high school-age daughter, Dena, to come with me. Initially, she agreed to come but then she changed her mind. I drove to the store, bought what I needed and started to return home, after buckling my seat belt as usual. As I entered the intersection of Glen Avenue and Park Heights Avenue, I realized that a car that had run the red light was racing toward me and was imminently going to hit the passenger side of my car. There was nothing I could do to avoid what was about to happen. My car was thrown to the other side of the street; the windshield cracked, and my hat and glasses were knocked off my head. *Baruch Hashem*, I was unharmed. Startled and shocked, I extended my right hand to check the extent of the damage. I quickly realized that the speeding car had smashed the front passenger side door and window, so that the door was now within twenty inches of me. Looking beyond the moment, I realized that had my daughter come along, she would have been sitting in that seat.

The *hashgachah pratis* was quite apparent after I thought back over the past few hours. I perceived that without the guiding Hand of Hashem, the results could have been quite tragic.

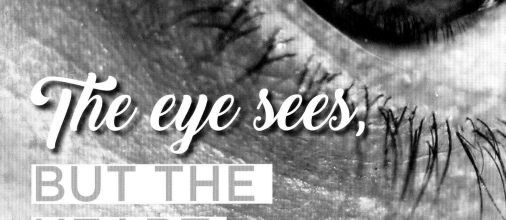

The eye sees,
BUT THE
HEART
PERCEIVES.

אוי להם לבריות שרואות ואינן יודעות מה הן רואות (חגיגה יב:)

Do You "Love" Fish?

Yaakov Avinu made a deal with Lavan Harasha. Yaakov would work seven years after which he would (ostensibly) marry Lavan's daughter, Rochel. The Torah informs us how quickly these seven years went by, stating that "they seemed to him like a few days because of his love for her" (*Bereishis* 29:20).

The Dubno Maggid queries why the reverse wasn't true. When one longs for something, time doesn't proceed quickly, rather it progresses slowly. The longer a person is deprived of what he wants, the greater his angst, and the more his impatience grows. A few days is then like a few years. Why then in Yaakov's situation, did the seven years seem like just a few days?

The Dubno Maggid explains this by distinguishing between actions that result from instinct, and those that result from reason. Instinctively, a person desires immediate pleasure and revolts at the thought of waiting. Then each additional minute that he is deprived of his selfish delight seems like an eternity. Behavior that is rooted in reason, however, focuses on its fulfillment, and then each day brings one closer to accomplishing one's goal. The Torah here is showing us that Yaakov Avinu's desire to marry Rochel was driven by reason and not by impulse. He knew that Rochel was chosen by Hashem to bring a share of the *shevatim* into the world. In order to elucidate Yaakov's altruistic motives, the Torah tells us that the seven years were but like a few days. Yaakov Avinu was driven solely by his desire to fulfill his mission in life.

Rav Eliyahu Lopian זצ"ל likens Yaakov's situation to a Jew who has no *tefillin* and is forced to create his own. Can one imagine his enthusiasm as each day passes and he prepares the skins, molds and dyes; the *batim* (boxes); prepares the *parshiyos* (scrolls); and forms and darkens the *retzuos* (straps)? Each day he is coming closer to the time that he will be able to fulfill his special mitzvah. Time doesn't lag; it accelerates as he sees his achievement closer at hand. This is because it is reason, rather than impulse, which is driving his actions.

Rav Lopian asks us to imagine a restaurant patron who orders fish because he "loves" fish. When the waiter brings the fish, the customer begins to devour it. The waiter questions the consumer and asks, "If you love the fish, why are you eating it?" Obviously he doesn't love the fish – he loves himself and wants to treat his own palate.

How can a person determine his true motives for loving something?

Today we use the term "love" very casually, not giving it any thought. We love our children and our children love ice cream. The difference is clear. The first is a selfless feeling while the second is driven by one's selfish cravings. This second implication may be at the root of a national Jewish problem, as we see the rate of assimilation skyrocketing. Each day more and more of our fellow Jews see no reason to perpetuate their Jewish birthright and proceed to marry gentiles.

In the early 1970s, I taught in a very special school. The Ezra Academy of Queens was established in 1968 when Jewish parents became disenchanted with public school education and decided to enroll their children in Jewish schools during a New York City public school strike. Traditional yeshivos could not accommodate these newcomers, and Ezra opened its doors. I had a student in one of my classes by the name of David Baker. David was a good student whose Jewish heart was very big, although he wasn't yet observant. After he graduated high school, he attended the University of Buffalo, working toward his B.A.

One day I received a letter from him. He wrote that although his studies were proceeding satisfactorily, he was shocked at the prevailing attitude among most of the Jewish college students. They would freely socialize with goyim without any consideration of their religious backgrounds. He wrote, "Being a Jew here is inconsequential. It's no more significant than one's political affiliation. Just as a Democrat would marry a Republican, so too a Jew would marry a non-Jew." He clearly articulated his deep dismay and disappointment.

I am happy to say that David's love for Eretz Yisrael led him there where he married a *frum* girl. At last report he is settled there and is raising his family committed to Torah and mitzvos.

Rav Eliyahu Dessler זצ"ל notes that in the center of the word אהבה (love) is הב, which is the Aramaic word for "give." Authentic "love" is rooted in giving; as in the mitzvah of loving Hashem or loving another Jew. Mistaken "love" is grounded in the drive to take pleasure and to satisfy one's own desire.

If you "love" the food you eat, "LOVE" IS MERELY A SELFISH TREAT.

כל אהבה שהיא תלויה בדבר, בטל דבר, בטלה אהבה (אבות ה, יט)

פרשת וישלח

An Eternal People

After having spent fourteen years in the yeshivah of Shem V'Ever and twenty years in Lavan's house, Yaakov was now preparing to meet his brother Eisav. On his way there, Yaakov was left alone, and a "man" wrestled with him. This "man," Rashi tells us, was the guardian angel of Eisav – the *sar shel Eisav*. Realizing that he would be unable to overcome Yaakov, the angel struck him on his thigh. Yaakov, however, grasped the angel and would not release him until the *malach* (angel) agreed to bless him. The *malach* then *bentched* him, saying that he will no longer be called Yaakov, but rather Yisrael, which expressed Yaakov's ability to overcome challenge. Yaakov then requested to know the *malach's* name but the response was simply, "Why do you ask my name?" This episode concludes as the Torah explains that Yaakov walked away limping, although he was later healed. Today we have a mitzvah not to eat an animal's *gid hanasheh* (sciatic nerve), since this was the spot where Yaakov was wounded.

What deep significance lies behind this incident? Why would the Torah relate all the particulars of this encounter, including the entire dialogue between Yaakov and the *sar shel Eisav*, unless it contained an eternal message?

The *Sefer Hachinuch* writes that this fight foreshadowed the struggle of the Jewish people until the coming of Mashiach. The *sar shel Eisav* was the embodiment of our enemy throughout history. In every generation there will be an enemy who is committed to destroying the Jewish people. However, just as this attacker was unsuccessful, our future adversaries will be unsuccessful, as well. Just like Yaakov was finally healed, so too, do we have faith that Hashem will eventually "heal us from our pain" upon the coming of Mashiach. The prohibition against eating the *gid hanasheh* is a constant uplifting reminder of Hashem's assurance to ultimately redeem us.

Perhaps we could add that when Yaakov asked for the name of his opponent, he was actually asking about his true identity. Yaakov realized that his rival represented the perpetual foe of his people. He wanted to be able to describe the enemy so that he could forewarn future generations. The *malach's* response was not forthcoming since our enemy's identity changes throughout history. There is no single prototype; each generation's threat carries a different face. And sometimes our enemy is even "faceless," as it is today in America; the insidious threat of assimilation.

How does our continuous survival attest to the veracity of the Torah?

As I was traveling to school one day in Los Angeles I pulled into a service station for some gas. As I was pumping gas, a huge tractor trailer pulled up in front of me. A burly driver then proceeded to pump gas into his massive truck. He looked at me and at the top of his lungs he screamed, "Are you Jewish?" I responded nervously in the affirmative. He then continued yelling, "Do you believe in G-d?" Again, I answered in the affirmative. Not letting up, he raised his voice above the noise of the traffic and shouted, "How do you know there is a G-d?" I was taken aback by his aggressive posture and didn't quite know how to respond. Recognizing how incongruous the scene must have looked, and understanding that a gas station was not the most conducive place for deep theological dialogue, I questioned him if he was Jewish. He replied that he was. I then inquired if he read history, to which he gave a negative response. I then raised my voice and yelled, "If there were no G-d, you and I wouldn't be here!" For the moment, the only sound one could hear was the drone of the traffic and then the click of the pump, signaling that my tank was full. The trucker then gave a loud and resounding groan, screaming, "Yeah!!"

This story has become part of our Pesach Seder, as we read how, "In each generation people rise up to destroy us, but Hashem delivers us from their hands."

Every Rosh Chodesh we recite Hallel. Hallel is generally reserved for praising Hashem for His miracles: On Pesach, for delivering us out of Egyptian slavery; on Shavuos, for miraculously receiving His Torah; and on Sukkos, for preserving us in the Wilderness. For what miracle do we recite Hallel monthly? Rabbi Samson Raphael Hirsch writes that it is the miracle of the continuous survival of the Jewish people. As the moon completes its monthly cycle around the earth and renews itself, so too, do we remember the miracle of our renewal.

The Jewish presence on earth serves as the conscience of the world. Our preservation as a nation attests to the existence of an all powerful G-d. How else could a people, who represent less than 1 percent of the world population, and who are continually targeted for extinction, continue to exist? We have defied all statistics – to the bitter chagrin of our enemies.

The Jewish person may be tortured and killed as the enemy takes pleasure,

BUT THE JEWISH PEOPLE WILL LIVE ON FOREVER AND EVER AND EVER.

בכול דור ודור עומדים עלינו לכלותינו והקב"ה מצילנו מידם
(הגדה של פסח)

Do We Stand by Our Principles?

Yosef Hatzaddik was brought to Mitzrayim and was sold to Potiphar, a prominent attendant in Pharaoh's court. The Torah explains that Potiphar placed Yosef in charge of his entire household since Potiphar saw that Hashem was with him and that he was an *ish matzliach* (a successful person). It could have been easy for Yosef, in such a position of importance, to become arrogant and even justify a lapse of moral discernment. Yet, Yosef is the paragon of unparalleled integrity. He is a man who is unwilling to compromise his high standards of morals and ethics under the most tempting of circumstances. When Potiphar's wife lures Yosef to be immoral, his reaction is swift and unbending. He would not betray his master's trust, nor would he sin against Hashem. Yosef's sense of integrity would not allow him to fall for the machinations of Potiphar's wife.

The Gemara (*Brachos* 61b) says that tzaddikim (righteous people) are ruled by their *yetzer hatov* (good inclination), whereas *resha'im* (wicked people) are ruled by their *yetzer hara* (evil inclination). Yosef is therefore referred to as "Yosef Hatzaddik." His demonstration of moral strength earned him the eternal appellation of "Hatzaddik." Often we are attracted to follow a questionable trail which may tempt us to compromise our principles. Let's not fall, by remembering how high Yosef stood.

What principles will you never compromise?

Rav Aharon Feldman שליט"א, Rosh Yeshivah of Yeshivas Ner Yisroel, told the following story at the 2009 Torah Umesorah convention. The story contrasts two individuals: one who lived with integrity and one who didn't, and the stark differences that resulted from their respective actions.

A devoted *menahel* hired an assistant to help him run the school. Unfortunately, within a short while, the assistant began to usurp the principal's authority, undermining him at every opportunity. The gratitude and cooperation which one would normally expect was totally lacking. The clash of power came to a head one day when the principal opened his office door to find the assistant sitting in his seat. Committed to the principle of peace and harmony, the principal turned around, never to return to his position. His commitment to *shalom* precluded a confrontation. When parents heard about this miscarriage of justice, they were outraged and wanted to intervene on behalf of the deposed principal. The principal did not allow them to do so, stating that even if he would win, the children would lose. The conflict would most certainly tear the school apart, and his number one priority was *shalom* – harmony.

As time went on, the principal who had left started a new yeshivah which grew and thrived. His excellent reputation spread and preceded him wherever he went. The former assistant, however, was removed within a short time amidst allegations and accusations of misappropriating funds. Shortly afterward, he tragically passed away at a relatively young age.

A person committed to virtuous behavior will not stumble and will always be able to stand tall before Hashem and before man.

If you stand for nothing

YOU FALL FOR EVERYTHING.

אם אין אני לי – מי לי? (אבות א, יד)

How Meaningful Are Our Dreams?

Parshas Mikeitz invariably coincides with Shabbos Chanukah. Is there any connection between the events of the *parshah* and the events of Chanukah? Rav Shimon Schwab זצ"ל writes that the answer can be found by trying to comprehend why Pharaoh was so troubled by his dreams. After all, aren't most dreams nonsense? Why was he so perturbed?

Rav Schwab writes that Pharaoh believed his dreams were the introduction of the threat of a new reality. If lean cows could devour robust ones, and if thin ears of grain could swallow healthy ones, then perhaps a mighty nation could be toppled by a meek one. If this was to be the case, how could Pharaoh rest assured that his fierce army could defeat an attacking force? It is for this reason that he was so disturbed, and this is why he welcomed Yosef's rather peaceful interpretation. We read this each year on Chanukah to reinforce the reality of our history, in which we see how Hashem delivered the mighty Yevanim into the hands of the weak Chashmona'im.

Sefer Bereishis is replete with dreams. In *Parshas Vayeitzei*, Yaakov dreams of angels going up and down a ladder as he is about to leave Eretz Yisrael. In *Parshas Vayeishev*, we learn how Yosef's two dreams incited his brothers' anger, and at the end of the *parshah*, we are told of the dreams of the chief butler and the chief baker. In this week's *parshah*, we are now introduced to Pharaoh's dreams.

How real are our dreams? Are they reflections or predictions of reality or just mumbo-jumbo? On the one hand, the Gemara says that all dreams contain some amount of nonsense (*Brachos* 55a). On the other hand, however, the Gemara says that dreams are a sixtieth of prophecy (*Brachos* 57b). And then from our *parshah* we learn that the actualization of a dream is determined by its interpretation. Based upon this, we are advised by our *chachamim* to relate distressing dreams to a good friend, who can then lend them a positive meaning. It seems that some dreams are to be treated seriously, while others are not.

The *Aruch Hashulchan* says that, "It is good for a person to accustom himself not to look into his dreams since most of them have no substance" (*Orach Chaim* 220, paragraph 4).

Are there dreams in your family that have become legend?

There are, however, dreams that are real and that carry a serious message. My father-in-law, Rav Eliyahu Meir Weinberger זצ"ל, was nine years old when his father died in Vienna, Austria. He, of course, said Kaddish during each *tefillah*. One night he had a dream which distressed him greatly. He dreamt that a man dressed in white with a long white beard came to him. He said, "Your father is hungry." The next night the dream repeated itself. He could not contain himself and decided to go to his uncle, hoping that he would be able to offer an explanation of the dream. His uncle shrugged the little boy off by saying, "It's nonsense, like most dreams are." However, the dream persisted, and it agitated the little Eliyahu Meir terribly. He decided to go to the *rav* of the shul. The *rav* took the dream very seriously and gave him an incredible explanation: "You are not enunciating each word in Kaddish clearly, and therefore, your father's soul is hungry." From that point onward, the young boy started to say Kaddish more slowly and clearly.

On one of the following nights, Eliyahu Meir again had a dream. This time the same old man with the long white beard appeared and said to my father-in-law, "Your father says thank you."

This story can send shivers down anyone's spine, but it has become part of the family lore. Not only does it speak volumes about the potential significance of a dream, but it also demonstrates the power that the Kaddish embraces.

Incidentally, the potency of Kaddish lies in the fact that it is an opportunity for a parent to cause the *Shem Shamayim* (Heavenly Name) to be sanctified after his/her death. Sanctifying G-d's name is the purpose of creation. This is alluded to by the fact that the first *pasuk* in the Torah and the *Yehei Shmei rabba* response to Kaddish both contain equal numbers of words and letters (seven words, twenty-eight letters). The *Aruch Hashulchan* thus states: "G-d forbid that a person should say Kaddish quickly and hastily since this is the way of ignorant people."

Dreams come and dreams go; which are real?

IT'S HARD TO KNOW.

אי אפשר לחלום בלא דברים בטלים (ברכות נה)

The Darkness of Galus

Yosef, having revealed himself to his brothers, assuages their guilt for having sold him as a slave. Yosef assures them that this is all part of Hashem's Master Plan to enable him to support them in Mitzrayim during the period of famine.

Pharaoh is also enthusiastic about the prospect of Yosef's family coming down to his country. What were Pharaoh's motives for wanting Yosef's family in Mitzrayim? The Seforno suggests that Pharaoh had hoped that by having Yosef's family live in Mitzrayim, Yosef would no longer think of himself as a foreigner and he would devote himself more to the interests of the country. The Ramban comments that the presence of Yaakov's prestigious family would reflect positively on Mitzrayim and on Yosef's aristocratic status.

Whatever the case may be, *Galus Mitzrayim* was about to commence. Yosef was keenly aware of the dangers of his family being influenced by, or absorbed into the Egyptian culture. Therefore, he "set the stage" by stating that his family were shepherds. Egyptians hated shepherds, since by the very nature of their work, they subjugated sheep, which the Egyptians worshipped. Pharaoh would therefore welcome Yosef's request for his family to live apart from the Egyptian population by settling them in Goshen. Yosef wanted to distance his family from the Egyptian way of life, so that they would not be under their sphere of influence.

The challenge of living in *galus* is even greater now than it was then. Today we no longer live apart from the goyim, but rather among them. We must work diligently to safeguard and promote our traditional values and moral upright character. It is incumbent upon us to ward off the clamor and dazzle of current societal mores which threaten *kedushas Am Yisrael*.

How does the darkness of today's *galus* affect you?

My father ע"ה earned an honest living as a businessman from the time he arrived in New York from Germany in 1938. In 1962, my father received a very lucrative offer from his company. The position, however, would require him to relocate our family to Vienna, Austria for one year. Before my parents would seriously consider such a possibility, they looked into the options for Jewish education. Jewish life in Vienna was minimal and there were few suitable schools. My older brother, however, was finishing high school and was planning to go to yeshivah in Eretz Yisrael anyway. For me, my parents located an Orthodox boarding school in the southwest area of Switzerland, 500 miles away. The greater concern was for my two elementary school-age sisters, who obviously could not leave home. My parents decided that for one year my sisters could receive their general education in Vienna in a secular English-speaking school, designed for children of American diplomats. This they would supplement with a private tutor for their Jewish studies.

With all the arrangements in place, our family scattered to three countries in two continents. My father's business venture was highly successful and the year passed quickly. Toward the end of the year, my father was informed by his firm that if he chose not to continue in Vienna they would have no position for him in their company.

At that point, my parents made a critical decision. They decided to return with the family to New York, despite the lack of a foreseeable income. They could not allow the family to continue to be exposed to non-Jewish influences. In addition to strong family roots, they knew that a vibrant Torah community was crucial to the healthy growth of our family. In a letter that was uncovered in 2019, my father wrote to my mother, "If we would continue to live here for many years there would be no way back... our family's bonds would break apart and it would ruin ours and our children's Yiddishkeit. Nothing could compensate for that."

Today, our *mesorah* is being impassionedly transmitted to a second, third and fourth generation, attesting to the wisdom behind their decision.

GALUS IS DARK, TORAH IS LIGHT.

*We need its rays
to see what's right.*

והאר עינינו בתורתיך ודבק לבנו במצותיך (ברכת קריאת ש...)

Humility as a Driving Force

When Yosef is told that his father Yaakov is sick, he brings his two sons, Menashe and Efraim, to be *bentched* by their grandfather, Yaakov. Despite Yosef's efforts that Yaakov give priority to his older son, Menashe, Yaakov insists on placing Efraim first, stating that he shall become greater than Menashe. The Chafetz Chaim asks: what *zechus* (merit) did Efraim have to be given this pre-eminence?

The answer can be found in the previous *pesukim*. Here Yaakov crosses his hands so that Efraim, who was on his left side, would receive the *brachah* from Yaakov's right hand. The Torah comments regarding Efraim: והוא הצעיר – *and he was the younger one*. The Chafetz Chaim explains that these words could also mean that he was the one who made himself small. Despite the prominence that Efraim experienced, he still remained humble. This, explains the Chafetz Chaim, was Efraim's unique *zechus* which earned him subsequent generations of greatness.

What really is humility? Is it a game of self-deception whereby a person denies his true accomplishments or refuses to recognize his real value? Is it an attitude of worthlessness that one places on himself and on his achievements? Nothing could be further from the truth! Rather it is the realization that Hashem has given each person unique abilities, albeit with limitations, so that he has the tools he needs in order to accomplish his mission in life. When he succeeds, he feels good that he has used his G-d-given talents productively, but he dare not boast, knowing that it is Hashem who has given him his special *kochos*.

Humility is that driving force which recognizes the Divine source of potential and which obligates a person not to waste any part of it. Each individual has a right to feel special without feeling better than the next person. Everyone, after all, has his or her individual mission. This is why *Chazal* emphatically tell us that every person must say, בשבילי נברא העולם – *The world was created for me*.

What acts of humility have you seen in others?

Rabbi Dr. Joseph Breuer זצ"ל, the illustrious grandson of Rabbi Samson Raphael Hirsch, came from Germany to the shores of America in February 1939. What he was able to accomplish in twenty years, few people could have accomplished in a lifetime. With vision, brilliance, determination and patience, he transplanted the Frankfurt *kehillah* to Washington Heights. Step by step, he worked tirelessly, encouraging and inspiring weary German refugees, bereaved of their families and friends by World War II. Rav Breuer followed the blueprint of Rav Hirsch in engineering a total *kehillah*, complete with *mikvah*, *chevra kadisha*, kashrus, *beis din* and, of course, a yeshivah and shul. His was to be a *kehillah* independent of all others, and every nuance of the Frankfurt-Am-Main *kehillah* in Germany would remain intact.

I was a young man of twenty-three, preparing for my *chasunah*, and I had a document which needed to be signed by Rav Breuer. Even though I had learned in his yeshivah through *beis midrash*, I had never had a private audience with Rav Breuer. I would now have to present myself and make my request to this venerated figure, who was then in his late eighties. I was very nervous. I called his daughter, Mrs. Meta Bechhofer, who told me when her father would be available. When I arrived, I was brought into Rav Breuer's study where he was learning at his desk. As I walked in, I witnessed a display of humility which I will never forget. Rav Breuer raised himself from his seat, despite his frail and aged condition, out of respect for me. Could it be that this *gadol*, who was almost four times my age, the individual who built the *kehillah* from scratch, the one whose Torah permeated every fiber of his body, would stand for a *yeshivah bachur*? After a brief conversation (in my very limited German), he slowly signed the document and wished me well.

Rav Breuer emulated his Creator, about Whom it is said, "Wherever you find His greatness, there you will find His humility."

"בשבילי נברא העולם"

I am the one
from whom
Hashem expects
something special.

כל אחד ואחד חייב לומר בשבילי נברא העולם (סנהדרין לז.)

When It's Good to Be Picked On

Hashem spoke to Moshe Rabbeinu for seven days, convincing him to accept his role as emissary to Pharaoh. Moshe Rabbeinu was reluctant to accept the position. He felt that since he had a speech impediment, he would not be able to communicate effectively. Ramban adds that Moshe felt that it would not be in Hashem's honor to send an ambassador who could not make a proper presentation.

Why didn't Moshe *daven* to be cured of his speech defect? Ramban offers two explanations: Firstly, Moshe wanted to maintain his disability since he hoped that this would disqualify him as Hashem's agent. In addition, Moshe's oral handicap originated from a miraculous event, which he viewed as a badge of honor. According to the midrash, this event occurred when Moshe, as a small child being raised in Pharaoh's palace, took the king's crown and placed it on his own head. This episode supported the theory of Pharaoh's magicians who said that this boy would one day redeem the Jewish people and destroy Pharaoh's kingdom. Other advisors said that the act was meaningless child's play. As a test, a tray with gold and a hot coal was placed before Moshe to see how deliberate his behavior was. When he was about to grab the gold, an angel came and pushed his hand. Moshe grasped the hot coal and placed it in his mouth, resulting in an injury to his tongue.

The overriding question, however, is why did Hashem want to send an imperfect messenger? The answer, says the Ran (ן"דרשת הר), is to teach us that *Hashem does not need man to be perfect in order for him to succeed. Hashem assists those people whom He chooses.* Our job is only to be deserving of His support, and *He* will then "equip" us for success.

How did Hashem equip someone who you know for success?

Rabbi Naftoli Neuberger ל"זצ arrived in America in March of 1938, at the young age of nineteen. His strong German accent, combined with the challenge of learning a new language, should have been a major obstacle toward achieving his lofty goals. Already in the early 1940s, while World War II was raging, he embarked on a major building campaign, directing the construction of Yeshivas Ner Yisroel at 4411 Garrison Boulevard. According to the Tribute Journal, distributed at the memorial dinner in 2006, this feat was just about miraculous: "It is astonishing to comprehend how a German refugee who had not yet fully mastered English, and for whom any travel required special permits, was able to overcome the system of rationing to obtain steel, bricks and all the other materials needed to build what was then a state-of-the-art yeshivah building."

Yeshivas Ner Yisroel's continued expansion and growth on Mount Wilson Lane in 1968 were only part of Rabbi Neuberger's success. Rabbi Neuberger was the one who labored intensively to open America's doors to Iranian Jewry when the Shah was overthrown and replaced with the radical Islamic Khomeini regime in 1979.

Another unpublicized episode reflecting the favor which Rabbi Neuberger gained in a wide range of circles occurred in the late 1990s. Rabbi Ari Neuberger, then President of Bais Yaakov, was working feverishly to purchase the site that the middle school was renting from the Sisters of Mercy since 1994. It seemed that all requests and offers were being ignored. Our school president asked his cousin, Rabbi Naftoli Neuberger (who was instrumental in bringing Rav Ari into this country), if he could intervene. Rabbi Naftoli Neuberger proceeded to contact Cardinal William Keeler, the Archbishop of Baltimore, with whom he had a special relationship. Within a month, Bais Yaakov and the Sisters of Mercy came to a mutual understanding regarding the sale of the property.

Rabbi Naftoli Neuberger understood that he owed his life's success to his Creator. I once was sitting at a community dinner with Rabbi Neuberger and ט"יבלח Mr. Jerry Kadden, Ner Yisroel's Executive Director. I asked the former how he knew that Mr. Kadden, who was hired as a *bachur*, was the right person for the job. He humbly replied, "When you are working *l'shem Shamayim* you have *siyatta d'Shmaya* (Divine assistance)."

HASHEM DOESN'T HAVE TO PICK PEOPLE WHO ARE EQUIPPED;

He simply equips those who are picked.

בא לוטהב מסייעים אותו (שבת קד.)

פרשת וארא

Becoming Great

Greatness is often confused with fame. We see from our *parshah* how one is totally unrelated to the other.

The Torah states, *This is Aharon and Moshe to whom Hashem spoke to take Bnei Yisrael out of Mitzrayim*. Rashi comments that at times Aharon's name precedes Moshe's, and at times it's reversed. This is to teach us, continues Rashi, that "They are equal as one."

Rav Moshe Feinstein זצ"ל asks the obvious question. Moshe was our greatest Navi, and through him the Torah was given. How is it possible that Aharon was equal to Moshe? Rav Moshe presents two answers. Firstly, even though they were not equal in stature, since Moshe could not have performed his mission without Aharon, they were equal, as they complemented each other.

His second answer speaks volumes about the definition of greatness. Aharon was equal in greatness to Moshe since the former realized his potential, just as Moshe realized his. It is irrelevant that Moshe's potential was greater than Aharon's. What matters is that they both lived the fullest lives that they could have, given their G-d-given potential. And when a Jew lives up to his potential, he is great, even though he may not be famous. This is consistent with what Hashem told Shmuel Hanavi, *"For man only sees through his eyes, but Hashem sees to the heart"* (Shmuel I 16:7).

The word ישראל is an acronym for יש ששים רבוא אותיות לתורה – *there are 600,000 letters in the Torah*. Since the number of men who left Egypt was also 600,000, each letter thus represents one Yid who left Mitzrayim. Each one of us, as their descendants, is counted through a letter in the Torah. Rav Gedaliah Schorr זצ"ל comments that just like a kosher *sefer Torah* needs every letter complete, so does Klal Yisrael need every Jew complete, i.e. having fulfilled his or her potential. We as a people are deficient if even one individual falls short of what he or she could accomplish.

We can now appreciate why the Maharal says that the letters of אדם are the same as the word מאד, much. Man has the potential to do much for himself and much for his people.

> **What steps can you take toward reaching your potential?**

In 1994, our last year in Los Angeles, my wife and I taught in the Etta Israel Center. We taught special children between the ages of eight and thirteen each Sunday morning. All the children came from religious homes, but due to their physical and emotional limitations, they could not attend Jewish schools. Sunday was their chance to be inspired by the spirit and beauty of Yiddishkeit. The lessons would obviously have to be "distilled" so that their Jewish souls could revel in spirituality despite their handicaps.

Music was a major medium which we employed. We *davened* and sang meaningful Hebrew and English songs to convey the beautiful *hashkafos* of our *Torah Hakedoshah*. But what were to be our educational goals? What realistic promise did these children possess? We were directed to be practical and not to expect them to learn past the first few letters of the *Aleph-Beis*. Imagine how amazed we were at the end of the year, when many of the children knew most of the Hebrew alphabet. They had exceeded our expectations and were certainly considered "great" in Hashem's eyes. My wife says, "Never put a 'ceiling' on children; we never know how much they can truly accomplish." Let's not shortchange any of our children.

The importance of individualizing goals, depending on personal aptitude and talent, is brought out best through this famous story, as related by Mr. Irving Bunim ז"ל, the past lay leader of American Orthodoxy: A certain Reb Zushe used to say that there was only one question which he feared on the final day of judgment: "If I am asked why I am not as great as Moshe Rabbeinu, I will answer that I did not have the mind nor the *emunah* nor the opportunity which he had. If I am asked why I am not as great as the Vilna Gaon, I will respond that I was not given his abilities. After all, he memorized the Gemara backward and forward. But the one question I fear," Zushe would say, shaking his finger, "is, 'Why were you not the Zushe that you could have been? Why did you not live up to your own capabilities and potential?'"

You can be like Moshe Rabbeinu but one thing is essential, KEEP CLIMBING AND STRIVING TO REACH YOUR POTENTIAL.

הוא אהרן ומשה (ו, כו)
לומר לך ששקולין כאחד (רש"י)
דכיון דאהרן עשה כל ימיו בשלימות כל רצון השי"ת שהיה
אפשר לו לעשות הוא שקול כמשה (הרה"ק הרי"מ משה)

When Quantity Does Count

Before Hashem brought the tenth and final plague on the Mitzriyim, He commanded Moshe and Aharon regarding the mitzvah of *Korban Pesach*, the Pesach offering. There are about ten additional mitzvos connected to this mitzvah. According to the *Sefer Hachinuch*, each one is intended to help us remember the miracle of *Yetzias Mitzrayim* – the exodus from Egypt. Why do we need so many mitzvos, all for the same purpose? Wouldn't one have sufficed?

The *Sefer Hachinuch* sets forth a cardinal principle in answering this question: האדם נפעל כפי פעולותיו – *a person is shaped by his actions*. The more a person is actively involved in the performance of a positive act, the greater will be the effect upon him. It is thus necessary for the Torah to multiply the מצות מעשיות (the operative "hands-on" mitzvos) regarding *Yetzias Mitzrayim* in order to thoroughly drive home its significance – the creation of Hashem's Chosen People.

We see the same concept in *Pirkei Avos* (3:19) where it states, *The world is judged with goodness and everything depends on the abundance of good deeds* (והכל לפי רב המעשה). From this, Rambam learns that the more one is invested in the performance of mitzvos, the greater the personal impact. Therefore, it is preferable, for example, for the giver to distribute ten single dollars, rather than to give one ten-dollar bill. Each dollar is an exercise in giving, and the effect is thus more embracing. Only through the repetition of such acts can a person be transformed from a taker to a giver; from an insensitive person to a compassionate individual.

Chazal also tell us, רצה הקב"ה לזכות את ישראל לפיכך הרבה להם תורה ומצות – *Hashem wished to confer merit upon Yisrael; He therefore gave them Torah and mitzvos in abundance*. Quantity definitely counts.

In the first *parshah* of Shema we precede the mitzvah of teaching Torah to our children by stating that the words of Torah should be על לבבך – on your heart. Why doesn't it say בלבבך – in your heart? I once heard that the only way to influence our children in Torah is to make sure that our hearts are overflowing with an abundance of Torah – on our hearts; beyond that which is in our hearts.

In the next *parshah* we'll learn what role the quality of a mitzvah plays.

How can you increase the quantity of mitzvos which you perform daily?

Mrs. Sugar* was a non-observant Jew, married with two children. She had everything that a person could want, including her own plane. The only thing lacking was happiness; her life was devoid of meaning. Unfortunately, her husband, Mr. Sugar, did not have that problem; he did not feel that spiritual vacuum. Mrs. Sugar, longing for a deeper meaning to her Jewishness, connected with Rabbi Avraham Chaim Lapin זצ"ל, in San Jose, California. His classes were stimulating and inspiring, adding a welcome dimension to her life.

Mrs. Sugar, now realizing that this is what she was looking for, proceeded to engage her children in her religious endeavors. Although she was unsuccessful with her teenage daughter, she convinced her son Benjamin* to go to a religious summer camp on the East Coast. There was just one problem. He needed a pair of *tefillin*, and Mr. Sugar refused to spend a penny to advance any step toward Jewish observance. In a monumental display of heartfelt determination, and a deep-seated commitment, she sold her wedding ring. She sent her son off with the necessary funds to a religious uncle in New York, who purchased the *tefillin* and taught Benjamin how to wear them, before going to camp.

After camp, Benjamin's mother persuaded him to attend YULA, where I was the principal. His resistance to the limits and expectations of the yeshivah required, at times, his mother's emotional intervention. Mrs. Sugar's eagerness to see her son religious was unwavering as she continued to gently push him in the right direction.

Mrs. Sugar was sadly forced to leave her husband, who would not respect his wife's religious lifestyle. She relocated, abandoning all her wealth, and moved into a rented apartment next door to us in Los Angeles, becoming a regular Shabbos guest and a cherished friend. Mrs. Sugar savored the opportunities to perform the will of Hashem through His bounty of mitzvos, thus inspiring Benjamin to continue learning in Eretz Yisrael after he graduated high school. A short time later, he married and established a religious home of his own in Los Angeles.

Fast forward twenty-eight years. Benjamin's children have gone through yeshivah, and ironically, he is sitting on the Board of Trustees of the same school which he initially resisted attending. More recently, Mr. Sugar tragically passed away in Northern California. Before he died, Benjamin told his father that he wanted to give him a religious burial. His father happily accepted the offer.

Thanks to Mrs. Sugar, Benjamin was able to send his father off with a gift that Mr. Sugar never wanted Benjamin to have.

*Name has been changed

Use Torah as your steering wheel, NOT AS A SPARE TIRE.

(Rabbi Yaakov Hopfer)

בכל דרכיך דעהו (משלי ג, ו)

Improving the Quality of a Mitzvah

Regretting that he allowed the Jewish people to leave Mitzrayim, Pharaoh and his forces pursued Bnei Yisrael. Once again, the Torah informs us that "Hashem hardened Pharaoh's heart," giving Pharaoh the resolve to chase after the Jewish people despite the previous punishments.

How could Hashem tamper with Pharaoh's free-will? How could Hashem blame Pharaoh for doing evil against His people if He Himself made Pharaoh's heart hard? Among various answers to this complex question is the approach of the Malbim. His response elucidates the nature of free-will, in contrast to forced-will. After Pharaoh was assailed with the *makkos*, he was no longer free but rather forced to let Bnei Yisrael go. In order to restore his *bechirah chafshis* (free-will), Hashem had to "inject" him with a strong dose of stubbornness. Pharaoh's choice to chase Bnei Yisrael was a deliberate decision, now that the balance of free-will was recalibrated.

Based on a person's level of consciousness, Hashem either rewards or, *R"l*, punishes a person. Is a mitzvah performed out of habit considered a conscious act? Is a mitzvah which is done robotically, or a *brachah* which is said mindlessly, considered a mitzvah? The Navi Yeshayah (29:13) admonishes Klal Yisrael for performing mitzvos by rote (מצות אנשים מלומדה) by stating that: *"With their mouths and lips they have honored Me but their heart was distant from Me."* We see that the Navi is dissatisfied with simple lip-service, although the mitzvah may technically have been fulfilled.

Interestingly, the Malbim lends a novel application. He says that the above *pasuk* refers to a person raised religiously, who performs mitzvos just as he saw them at home, but perceives the mitzvos as orders from his parents rather than commandments of G-d.

Rav Meir m'Premishlan once said that we need to achieve in our *avodas Hashem* (Divine service) an element of personal devotion, while carrying within us the traditions of our fathers. This is alluded to in this week's *shiras hayam* where it states, זה קלי ואנוהו – *this is my G-d and I will glorify Him*, followed by, אלקי אבי וארממנהו – *the G-d of my father and I will exalt Him*.

We can raise the quality of our mitzvos if, when performing a מִצְוָה (commandment), we allow the מְצַוֶה (Commander) to enter our hearts. The only thing it takes, is for us to "soften" our hearts and to bring the mitzvos closer to our minds.

> **What can you do to "connect your mind to your heart"?**

It was during my earlier years of school administration when I left school one day feeling very despondent.

I came home and headed straight for the kitchen. No, not to eat, but to do something different. I wanted to drive away the unfulfilling events of the day and to get busy with something I had never done. I decided to bake a cake. Deflecting all my wife's questions, I took out a recipe book, prepared the necessary ingredients, and began working. Everything looked pretty simple: one cup of sugar, one half teaspoon of salt, three cups of flour, one cup of water, etc., place in the oven for forty-five minutes at 350°. What could go wrong?

After forty-five minutes, I eagerly returned to retrieve the results of my anticipated successful "experiment." I opened the oven door, and, lo and behold, it looked the same as when I had put it in. I quickly realized my mistake. I had neglected to turn the oven on!

After I recovered from this fiasco, I said to myself that herein must lie some deep lesson: Without warmth, despite the proper ingredients, little, if anything, can be accomplished. One can *daven*, say all the words, *shuckel* and go through all the motions of fulfilling any mitzvah, but without the warmth of the heart, the true product of the mitzvah will not be achieved. That product is the building of the quintessential Jew.

Chazal say, לא נתנו המצות אלא לצרף בהן את הבריות – *Mitzvos were only given to refine people*. The desired outcome of living a life of mitzvos is the formation of an ideal human being. Mitzvos can transform a Jew, but only if he "turns on the heat"; if he realizes that he is fulfilling the desire of his Creator. Performing a mitzvah out of habit falls short of what Hashem wants and denies our *neshamah* the sustenance that it needs.

The story is told of a rebbe who always gave *tzedakah* very generously. Then for three months he stopped. When asked why, he responded that when he saw a Jew in need, he felt compelled to give. He realized that he was no longer in control of his giving, and he wanted to regain control so that it would be a conscious mitzvah.

Although the mind is but a foot from the heart, AT TIMES THEY MAY SEEM TO BE MILES APART.

וִידַעְתָּ הַיּוֹם וַהֲשֵׁבֹתָ אֶל לְבָבֶךָ (דברים ד, לט)

פרשת יתרו

One Symphony

Bnei Yisrael, having now arrived at Har Sinai, were preparing to receive the Torah. The *pasuk* states, ויחן שם ישראל נגד ההר – *and Yisrael encamped there opposite the mountain*. The word ויחן is in the singular form, in contrast to the previous words, which are all in plural form. Rashi notes that this teaches us that as Bnei Yisrael surrounded the mountain they were as a single person, with a single desire, כאיש אחד בלב אחד. It seems that unity was essential in order to receive Hashem's most precious gift. Why was solidarity a prerequisite to receiving the Torah?

Rav Chaim Shmuelevitz זצ"ל explains that although the Torah speaks to each individual, it was given to the Jewish nation as a whole. In order to qualify as a nation there had to be total unity; a oneness of body and a joining of spirit. Perhaps one could add that the Torah was given to the Jewish nation as a whole since no one person can fulfill the entire Torah. Some mitzvos are unique for *kohanim*, some for *levi'im*, and some are specific for women. Some mitzvos are also "position specific" – for example, the King of Yisrael. Since the purpose of Torah is to fulfill its mitzvos, only as one nation can we keep the entire Torah.

This oneness challenges us to promote *achdus* (unity) through the way we talk to and act toward our fellow Jews. We are part of One People and as such we are responsible for one another. This is why the overwhelming part of our *davening* is in the plural form: סלח לנו (forgive us); רפאנו (heal us); שמע קולנו (hear our voice); ותחזנה עינינו (may our eyes see).

There are behaviors, however, which undermine our calling. Divisiveness, *lashon hara*, jealousy and hatred are ingredients which poison our position of strength. Is there any wonder why *sinas chinam* (warrantless hatred) was the cause for the destruction of our second Beis Hamikdash? Its purpose as a place of service for His one people was negated when our actions contradicted our essence.

The *Midrash Tanchuma* in *Parshas Nitzavim* states that the *Geulah* will come only when we act as one group – אגודה אחת. Let's work to make this a reality.

What can you do to promote *achdus*?

When discussing the unity of the Jewish people, Rav Shimon Schwab זצ"ל made sure to underscore a glaring enigma. We are One People, yet Jews are so different from one another. We have Chassidim, Misnagdim, Sephardim, Ashkenazim and many more groups – each with its own specific way of *davening* and each with its own unique Hebrew pronunciation. How can there be such differences within one nation?

Rav Schwab would explain that in reality the Jewish People is *one symphony*. The beauty of an orchestra lies in its diverse instruments (woodwind, string, percussion...), which together create sounds of harmonious music. No player is jealous of the mastery of his neighbor since he realizes that the "whole" can succeed only through each individual's success. So too, each Yid is required to respect and welcome the next person's "music." But these harmonic sounds can only come together when each member follows the maestro. So too, as long as we follow the "One Conductor," the collective sound which resonates is nothing short of majestic.

In *davening* we continuously request of Hashem to see us as part of one people – ברכנו אבינו כלנו כאחד – *bentch us, our Father, all as one*. In *bentching* we also say, כן יברך אותנו כלנו יחד – *so He should bentch us all together*. We want to be seen as part of one special entity. We must make sure that our behaviors support and not contradict that which we are asking from Him.

Feeling responsible to bring Yidden back to Yiddishkeit is one of the greatest expressions of *achdus*. Rav Simcha Wasserman זצ"ל was busy building his yeshivah for twenty-five years in Los Angeles. Yet he toiled tirelessly to learn with non-*frum* Jews and inspired them to become religious.

In the 1950s, my father ע"ה influenced a very special couple to become religious. Years later members of our family came together in Washington Heights with this couple and with members of their family. They wanted to thank us for my parents' friendship which was the cause of four generations (currently) being committed Jews. One never knows how far the ripples of Torah extend.

It is especially during times of peril that we see this "*achdus* imperative" spring into action. We saw it during WWII, when the Vaad Hatzalah was created to save Jewish lives. We see it today in Baltimore, and in every other Jewish metropolis when *gemachs*, Hatzalah, Chaverim and Shomrim relieve any person in need. Let's individually promote this attitude in our daily living.

מי כעמך ישראל – *Who is like Your people, Yisroel*,

גוי אחד בארץ – *one nation in the land*.

פרשת משפטים
Refined Justice

The *Torah Hakedoshah* demands that we, being Hashem's Chosen People, demonstrate respect. This respect goes beyond the behavior that we show toward other people, since it extends to their property as well. This is shown by how we treat items that are not ours, and the sense of responsibility which we display when we use someone else's items, even with permission.

But how Divine are these "rules," these mitzvos, which govern our behavior toward property which isn't ours? From the very first letter of *Parshas Mishpatim* we see that their origin is as G-dly as any pronouncement in the *Aseres Hadibros* (Decalogue). Rashi comments that this *parshah* begins with the letter *vav* ("and these are the laws") which connects the *Aseres Hadibros* of the previous *parshah* to ours. Just like the "Ten Commandments" were given by Hashem at Har Sinai, so too, were the social ordinances of this *parshah*.

But how are these laws different from the ordinances of any society which protect their neighbors' rights and property? The answer can be found through a careful study of the Preamble to the American Constitution: "We, the people of the United States, in order to form a more perfect *union*, establish justice, ensure domestic tranquility..." The founding fathers of this country were interested only in promoting law and order. They were not concerned with refining or creating moral, upstanding individuals. *L'havdil*, Hashem's *mishpatim* were designed to form a more perfect *individual* by directing him to exercise extraordinary discretion in his dealings with others; it is not simply a method of shackling an untamed beast.

Dovid Hamelech says in *Tehillim,* לא עשה כן לכל גוי ומשפטים בל ידעום – *He did not do like this for any other nation and our mishpatim they do not know.* The reason why the goyim do not "know" our ordinances is because ours is not simply a practical solution to prevent anarchy but rather a Divine system of developing good and moral character. In Jewish law, for example, there is no such thing as a "victimless crime." Any act which is morally wrong has at least one victim – the perpetrator himself. Alternatively, in civil law, each citizen is legally bound not to disseminate false information about another person, since he would be guilty of slander. In halachah, however, any (purposeless) negative information is sinful, regardless of whether it is true or not. The Torah's goal is to mold positive people and to prevent them from spreading gossip.

Rav Nisson Alpert זצ"ל explains that the Sanhedrin which judged all "wrongs" was placed next to the *Mizbei'ach* (altar). This teaches us that justice is as much *avodas Hashem* (Divine service) as was the *avodas hakorbanos* (sacrifices).

> **How is "distance yourself from dishonesty" different than "don't be dishonest"?**

How "lawless" can ordinary citizens become? How low can a normal society stoop? Anyone who was in Los Angeles on April 29, 1992, can easily answer that question. At that time, a jury in Los Angeles acquitted four white police officers accused in the videotaped beating of an African-American ex-convict, Rodney King. Thousands of people in Los Angeles rioted over the six days that followed the verdict. Widespread looting, assault, arson and murder occurred, and property damage toppled more than one billion dollars. In all, fifty-three people died during the riots and thousands more were injured. A store right around the corner from our home was set ablaze. It was the scariest time of our lives. Although the center of activity was downtown, the hooligans fanned out all over the city. Innocent drivers were pulled out of their cars and dragged to the ground. The city's residents were confined to their homes in the evening, due to a curfew. A *chasunah* that was scheduled for that evening was pushed ahead to take place during daylight hours in a neighbor's tennis court. Helicopters hovered overhead as a pervasive stench of burning ash filled the air.

Ordinary decency "went out the window" and man was reduced to a wild beast. Dialing 911 was futile since the response was a perpetual busy signal. Members of the *frum* community were forced to reflect on the sanctity of their own homes, when the safety of the *sifrei Torah* in the local shuls was called into question. Perhaps our homes would be less of a target for these hoodlums. But were our homes suitable for a *sefer Torah*?

The story is told of an individual who reported to Rav Shimon Schwab זצ"ל that a religious Jew was found guilty of corruption and was imprisoned. Rav Schwab asked him to repeat what he just said. Rav Schwab finally corrected the individual by saying, "He is not a religious Jew if he committed a crime and is sitting in jail."

Rabbi Dr. Joseph Breuer זצ"ל was known to say that being a religious Jew does not simply entail eating glatt kosher, it also means being *glatt yosher* (straight).

Law and Order is government's main assignment; **THE TORAH ALSO STRESSES PERSONAL REFINEMENT.**

לא נתנו המצוות אלא לצרף בהן את הבריות (בראשית רבה מד, א)

פרשת תרומה
Recipe for Life

There are no superfluous details in the Torah. Every word is Divinely measured and contains important lessons. Even the dimensions of the vessels in the Mishkan are recorded to convey an important message. The *Chumash* tells us that there were three vessels in the Mishkan that had a זר זהב סביב – a gold crown (trim) around them. They were the ארון (ark), שלחן (table) and מזבח הזהב (golden inner altar).

Their dimensions were as follows:

ארון – 1½ *amos* wide x 2½ *amos* long x 1½ *amos* high

מזבח הזהב – 1 *amah* wide x 1 *amah* long x 2 *amos* high

שלחן – 1 *amah* wide x 2 *amos* long x 1½ *amos* high

The Kli Yakar explains that these three vessels represent three distinct aspects of life. The ארון, which carried the *luchos* (the two tablets) represents *ruchniyus* (spirituality). All of its dimensions are mixed numbers, which contain a fraction. This is to teach us that in regard to our *avodah* (service to Hashem), we should never feel whole or satisfied. Rather, we should think that we have achieved only a fraction of our potential.

Concerning the מזבח הזהב, all the dimensions are whole numbers. The Kli Yakar explains that the *korbanos* (represented by the *Mizbei'ach*) bring a person to *teshuvah* (repentance), which leads to restoring our complete self. Thus, each measurement is a whole number.

The שלחן, which carried the twelve *lechem hapanim* (eaten by the *kohanim*), represents *gashmiyus*, physicality. Two of the three dimensions are whole numbers. This teaches us that in regard to our tangible goods, we are to be satisfied and we are to consider ourselves "whole" and "complete." The height, which does contain a fraction, is informing us how to feel content. We must split our desires and distinguish between our needs and our wants. Many times, luxuries become necessities and we begin to feel inadequate when we don't have them.

Training ourselves to be content with life's blessings is an exercise in recognizing good. Too often, we take the "little things" for granted and we are left with a feeling of discontent. Here is a tongue (mind)-twister which I once heard:

Why is it that we don't have what we want?

It's because we don't want what we have.

If we would want what we have,

Then we would have what we want.

What can you do to heighten your appreciation for the "little things"?

Rejoicing daily with our "mundane" blessings requires effort. We don't appreciate things, because we don't bother to think of them as anything special. I learned this lesson in 1988 on a trip to Communist Russia.

Three teachers (including myself) and eleven senior girls traveled from Los Angeles to Moscow and St. Petersburg (known then as Leningrad). Our mission was to deliver "contraband" – *tefillin*, *mezuzos*, siddurim, etc., to our deprived Jewish brothers and sisters behind the "Iron Curtain." Our journey spanned ten days, and in addition to the above "forbidden items," we needed to take along enough food for our group. We stuffed our duffel bags with canned foods and lots of jars of peanut butter, which is a convenient high-energy food.

Each day we visited Refuseniks (Jews who were refused permission to make *Aliyah*) who shared with us their dreams of one day living in Israel, being allowed to follow Hashem's Torah openly. Our admiration of these people soared as we saw how each group welcomed our sacred gifts with enormous joy. But this joy paled in comparison to the happiness which a few jars of peanut butter produced. Let me explain.

Toward the end of our trip we had extra jars of peanut butter. We decided to bring them along on our visits, since perhaps someone could use them. We entered a home and after exchanging niceties, the mother started to pour out her heart to us. Her young son was developing bowleggedness, a symptom of rickets, since he had stopped drinking milk, which is a source of vitamin D. She explained that he would not drink milk without any added flavor. What she said then still sends shivers down my spine, "...any kind of flavor would work – even peanut butter. You wouldn't happen to have any of that, would you?" We ran to our duffel bags and exposed our "gold." Her eyes lit up in disbelief. We were thrilled to be Hashem's agents to supply this family with what we thought was just excess baggage. This to us was not only a lesson in *hashgachah pratis*, but it also was a message never to take anything for granted.

Our challenge in life is to "relabel" our household items from "regular" to "special."

In gashmiyus be content with your fortune, IN RUCHNIYUS STRIVE FOR A GREATER PORTION.

קנאת סופרים תרבה חכמה (בבא בתרא, כא.)

In the opening *pesukim* of this week's *parshah*, Hashem commands Moshe to have the בגדי כהונה (priestly garments) fashioned for Aharon and his family. But to whom was Moshe to address this mandate? The Torah tells us that he was to direct his orders to all the חכמי לב – to all the wise-hearted people who were filled with the spirit of wisdom. In *Parshas Vayakhel*, as well, the Torah informs us that the women who were "wise-hearted" were directed to spin the thread from which the clothing was made. The obvious question is, why is wisdom associated with the heart as opposed to the mind? Shouldn't the Torah have written "wise-minded" as opposed to "wise-hearted"?

Rav Chaim Shmuelevitz זצ"ל explains that the Torah uses a precise term which describes the prerequisite necessary for full understanding: motivation. The degree that a person will comprehend depends on his drive to understand. If a person has little motivation, then he will not succeed in accessing his cerebral capacity. On the other hand, if he is determined to understand, then he will put in the necessary effort and he will tap into his mind's potential.

This drive, this desire, is rooted in the heart! We see this at the end of Shema where we say, ולא תתורו אחרי לבבכם – *do not go after (the drives of) your heart*. Since wisdom depends, to a large extent, on a person's attitude and determination, wisdom in Tanach is always connected to the heart as opposed to the mind. Thus, Hashem gave to Shlomo Hamelech a לב חכם ונבון (מלכים א יב:ג) – a wise and understanding heart. In *davening*, as well, we ask Hashem, ותן בלבנו להבין ולהשכיל – *put into our heart the ability to understand*. Additionally, at the end of *Shemoneh Esrei*, we ask Hashem, פתח לבי בתורתך – *open my heart to Your Torah*.

The key is to be able to cultivate within ourselves and within our children an attitude to want to learn, and to want to grow as a Jew. Therefore, it is easy to understand the sentiment that "I can" and "I will" are more important than I.Q.

What positive or negative attitudes contribute to your behavior?

Rav Shlomo Wolbe זצ"ל writes that cultivating proper attitudes in our children is an act of "planting." Just as when we sow seeds the results are not immediate, so too, the attitudes that our children have are usually a product of many years of cultivation. However, sometimes parents can send a strong, yet subtle message that can "jump-start" a dormant attitude, so that it quickly crystallizes in a child's heart. Such was the situation in which my daughter-in-law, Mrs. Shoshana Hexter, grew up.

When she was in high school, she would often participate in numerous activities with her friends, inside and outside of school. On one occasion, there was an organized trip to see the Ice Capades. This was to be a show on ice in which men and women, dressed "for the occasion," would skate doing all kinds of tricks, demonstrating thrilling acts of showmanship. A short time before the trip, her father, Rabbi Yehuda Naftoli Mandelbaum ז"ל, asked to speak with her. Rabbi Mandelbaum, being the master *mechanech* that he was (as well as a seasoned *rebbi* in Torah Institute), wanted to convey his feelings to his daughter about the trip. He said to her, "I just want you to know that the Ice Capades is a show which runs contrary to the attitudes which we want to develop in our children about *tznius* (modesty). I am not telling you not to go, but just consider this before you finalize your decision."

My daughter-in-law thought about it and decided that she would go with her friends. She left her home to meet her ride, but kept on thinking about her father's words. As she was about to knock on her neighbor's door, she turned back. Something "clicked." A new and lucid attitude toward *tznius* percolated in her mind, and she decided not to go. Had my *chashuve mechutan* forbade his daughter from going, she certainly would not have gone but she also would not have had the opportunity to adopt this critical way of thinking. This attitude took root in my daughter-in-law's heart and helped her appreciate a difficult concept. This enabled her to formulate an independent decision and contributed greatly to her growth.

It's your attitude,
not your aptitude,

**THAT DETERMINES
YOUR ALTITUDE.**

הקב"ה ליבא בעי דכתיב "וה' יראה ללבב" (סנהדרין קו:)

פרשת כי תשא
The Sign of Shabbos

Every Shabbos we reaffirm the words of this week's *parshah*:

ושמרו בני ישראל את השבת... ביני ובין בני ישראל אות היא לעולם – *The Bnei Yisrael shall observe the Shabbos... between Me and Bnei Yisrael, it is a sign forever."*

We proclaim that Shabbos is a sign that Hashem created the universe in six days, and that on the seventh day He rested. How is Shabbos a "sign"? The Chafetz Chaim explains that this "sign" is comparable to the shingle a craftsman hangs outside his home which identifies him according to his craft, e.g. a tailor, a shoemaker, etc. As long as that sign is hanging it is evident that the individual is still in business. Even if he leaves for vacation, the sign publicizes to everyone that this is still his place. Once the sign is removed, however, it becomes obvious that the owner has left. So too, continues the Chafetz Chaim, as long as the "sign of Shabbos" is present by a Jew, even if he may be delinquent in other mitzvos, he still identifies himself as a Jew – he is still "home." Once the placard of Shabbos has been removed, then his belief in Hashem and His Torah is compromised. He is no longer home.

Chazal say that observing Shabbos is tantamount to giving testimony that Hashem created the world. Rabbi Samson Raphael Hirsch זצ"ל explains this in the following way: Man shows his dominion over the earth by being able to "fashion all things in his environment for his own purpose." On Shabbos, by refraining from *melachah*, he "acknowledges that he has no rights of ownership or authority over the world... on each Shabbos the world, so to speak, is restored to G-d and thus man proclaims, both to himself and his surroundings, that he enjoys only a borrowed authority" (*Horeb* Vol. I pg. 63).

The above concept can be best understood through a parable. Malka entrusted her prized Lamborghini to Sarah while the former went on vacation. The only stipulation was that Sarah remember that the car was on loan to her and that it was not her own. Sarah agreed but since she had the freedom to use the car at will, she forgot that she was using a borrowed possession. When Malka got wind of this, she ordered Sarah to stop using her Lamborghini on Tuesdays. No longer did Sarah have the free rein that she had had previously. By curbing the car's use, Sarah was made to realize that the car was not hers, but only on loan. So too, Hashem limits our use over His world on Shabbos, to remind us that it is only on loan and it is not our own.

> **In what way can you enhance the "sign of Shabbos" in your home?**

Dr. Aharon Meir (Adolf) Lowenthal was a *frum* doctor in Germany. He was miraculously released by the Nazis ש"מי, in the early years of WWII, after which he came to this country. (He was so grateful for this that one could see tears well up in his eyes when he *bentched* the *Shehecheyanu* on every Yom Tov.) Despite the challenge of learning a new language, he successfully passed the medical boards here, and became a respected and accomplished urologist in New York. He was known not only for his medical prowess, but also for his expertise as a *mohel*. He was a true *yerei Shamayim* who would do anything to help a fellow Yid.

Thus, it was not surprising that when a young mother gave birth to her seven-and-a-half-pound son in the Central Maternity Hospital, the family wanted Dr. Lowenthal to be the *mohel*. There was just one problem. Since the baby was born on Shabbos, the eighth day would also be on Shabbos. This meant that the *bris* would have to be in the hospital, since at that time mothers convalesced in the hospital for about ten days. The hospital was located in the Bronx, and Dr. Lowenthal lived in mid-Manhattan, a distance of about ten miles. Would he be willing to trek this distance? Being the dedicated and selfless tzaddik that he was, he consented. He brought all his equipment before Shabbos and then walked the distance on a warm Shabbos morning in June. He performed the *bris*, after which he walked to nearby Washington Heights where he stayed until after Shabbos.

Dr. Lowenthal was blessed with lengthy days as he lived until the age of ninety-one. He continued to do *brissim* even when he was older, as he felt *bentched* that his hands continued to remain steady. *Chazal* say, אין הקב"ה מקפח שכר כל בריה – *Hashem does not withhold compensation from any individual for any good deed.* It seems that the ten miles that Dr. Lowenthal walked that Shabbos were paid back about fifty years later. That's when Dr. Lowenthal's grandson married the daughter of that seven-and-a-half-pound infant. I know – I was that baby.

On Shabbos
return the world
to its Owner;

AFTER ALL, IT'S
ONLY A "LOANER"

כל מי שמשמר את השבת מעיד על מי שאמר והיה העולם
(ילקוט שצ)

פרשת ויקהל

Elevated Wisdom

Dovid Hamelech in *Tehillim* (111:10) tells us that 'ראשית חכמה יראת ה – *the beginning of wisdom is the fear of Hashem*. Are we to understand that "fear" is a form of wisdom?

Rav Leib Chasman זצ"ל, quoted in the *Yalkut Lekach Tov*, explains that theoretical *chachmah* which has no practical application is not "wisdom." True *chachmah* is information which can transform a Yid into a better person. Theoretical knowledge simply stored in the mind is comparable, Rav Chasman continues, to a donkey carrying a load of *sefarim*. It has no effect on the quality or sophistication of the animal. A Jew, however, who is "saddled" with *yiras Shamayim*, realizes that what he learns and the capacity which he has to learn, must be used to bring him closer to Hashem. Thus the fear of Hashem is a prerequisite to true *chachmah*.

Yiras Shamayim is more a function of the heart than it is of the mind. The brain may be the reservoir for knowledge, but this material needs to be elevated through the heart so that it can be saturated with *yiras Shamayim*. Only then can *chachmah* be used to bring one closer to Hashem. This is what we mean each day when we say in *Aleinu*: וידעת היום והשבות אל לבבך – *you shall know this day and take to your heart (that Hashem, He is the G-d...).*

We now have another explanation (in addition to that which was explained in *Parshas Tetzaveh*) why Moshe Rabbeinu addresses the חכמי לב (wise-hearted people) in this week's *parshah*. After all, isn't *chachmah* the function of the mind? However, the technical ability to build the Mishkan and to sew the *bigdei kehunah* are secondary to the primary responsibility of its artisans, to imbue the sacred items with G-dliness. For this to be accomplished, one must employ men and women whose skill and depth of learning are consistent with their conduct. This can only be accomplished through people whose wisdom is elevated through their fear of Hashem, which rests in the heart.

> **How can a person tell if his wisdom has "reached" his heart?**

For many years Bais Yaakov of Baltimore had regular *Limudei Kodesh* classes for grades seven through twelve each Sunday morning. As time wore on, consideration was given to discontinuing the Sunday schedule, in step with most Bais Yaakovs in the country. Parents and teachers wanted more time to spend with family, and it was becoming more and more difficult to maintain regular attendance for students as well as for faculty. This major change, however, would not be considered unless the *roshei yeshivah* would be in agreement. After all, Bais Yaakov of Baltimore was conceived by spiritual luminaries such as Rav Shimon Schwab זצ"ל, with ongoing guidance from other *gedolei Yisrael* such as Rav Yaakov Yitzckok Ruderman זצ"ל, Rav Yaakov Kamenetsky זצ"ל and Rav Yitzchak Hutner זצ"ל. *Da'as Torah* would need to be consulted before decreasing the number of school days.

A meeting was set up in the late 1990s in Yeshivah Torah Vodaas with Rav Avraham Pam זצ"ל and להבחל"ח Rav Yaakov Perlow שליט"א (Novominsker Rebbe) and Rav Shmuel Kamenetsky שליט"א (who later had to cancel). Members of Bais Yaakov's Vaad Hachinuch, including its principals and president, Rabbi Ari Neuberger, made their presentation, assuring the *roshei yeshivah* that whatever time would be lost by dropping Sunday, would be made up on Friday, or by extending another day. Rav Pam זצ"ל interjected that a girl should never be kept in school longer on Erev Shabbos, since that is exactly when she should be home. At that point I questioned the necessity to recoup any lost hours of *Limudei Kodesh* since women have no obligation per-se to learn Torah – "it's only תלמוד תורה דנשים – the mitzvah of learning Torah for women." Rav Pam quickly retorted that it is to be considered יראת שמים דנשים – "the mitzvah to fear Hashem," which is also incumbent upon women. Rav Pam saw a Bais Yaakov education as an opportunity to impart *yiras Shamayim*. Fearing Hashem is as much of an obligation on women as it is on men.

Pursuant to this meeting, Bais Yaakov retained Sunday classes for several more years. About five years later another meeting was held, at which point it was decided to discontinue school on Sunday, while extending its Monday through Thursday schedule.

A Jew may be considered smart,

WHEN YIRAS SHAMAYIM IS IN HIS HEART.

ראשית חכמה יראת ה' (תהלים קא, י)

Being Faithfully Honest

Among the *bigdei kehunah* (priestly garments) worn by the *kohen gadol* was the אפוד. This garment was similar to an apron, onto which the חושן משפט (breast plate) was firmly attached on all four corners. The Torah states, ולא יזח החשן מעל האפוד – *and the breast plate will not be loosened from upon the* אפוד. In fact, the *Sefer Hachinuch* counts this as one of the 365 negative commandments in the Torah.

In explaining the possible rationale behind this mitzvah, the *Sefer Hachinuch* suggests that perhaps a shaky and loose חושן would disturb the beauty and dignity surrounding the priestly garments. Interestingly, the *Sefer Hachinuch* himself doesn't seem to be very satisfied with his own explanation and suggests that we accept it until a better one is heard.

Rav Moshe Feinstein זצ"ל does offer another explanation. He says that connecting the חושן and אפוד represents a philosophical association and not just a physical one. This is because each one of the garments worn by the *kohen gadol* atones for a specific communal sin. The חושן atones for dishonesty and the אפוד for *avodah zarah* (idol worship). *Avodah zarah* is a denial of Hashem and dishonesty is the result of denying Hashem's ability to sustain the individual. This then may be the lesson that Hashem is conveying. Dishonesty results from a lapse of true belief in Hashem.

The Gemara (*Shabbos* 104a) asks why, in the order of the Hebrew alphabet, are the letters of שקר (falsehood, dishonesty) found all together, whereas the letters of אמת (truth) are spread throughout the *Aleph-Beis*. The Gemara answers that this reflects a sad reality. Falsehood is common, and thus easily found. Truth and honesty, on the other hand, take more effort to locate, both in the *Aleph-Beis* and in the world at large.

If we would be continuously cognizant that we are in His hands, we would never doubt His ability and we would never sink into the despair which could lead to dishonest actions.

What would you tell a friend who you noticed cheating on a test?

Jeremy's grandfather was disturbed that his grandson was not growing up religiously. In an effort to inspire him to be observant, the grandfather bought him an expensive pair of *tefillin* for his bar mitzvah. In response to his grandfather's continuous pleas for commitment, Jeremy respectfully agreed to don his *tefillin* every weekday.

Summertime approached and Jeremy was packing his bags to go to camp. Grandpa handed Jeremy the *tefillin* bag, reminding him to wear them each day in camp. A week later Grandpa received a letter from Jeremy saying that all was well in camp but he needed some cash. A few days later Jeremy received a return letter from Grandpa containing just seven words: "Did you put on your *tefillin* today?" Disappointed that no cash was forthcoming, Jeremy responded in his next letter by saying: "Yes, I put on my *tefillin* today. Please send cash." A week later the same seven words were communicated: "Did you put on your *tefillin* today?" This once again sparked an irritated response: "Yes, I did. Please send cash." Once again Jeremy got the same seven-word response.

The camp season came to a close, and waiting for Jeremy at the bus was his grandfather. As Jeremy alighted from the bus, he gave his grandfather a cold kiss and demanded to know why he hadn't sent any money. "Why did you just keep on asking me if I put on my *tefillin*?" His grandfather asked to see the *tefillin* bag, and he tenderly opened the zipper, exposing a fifty-dollar bill sitting neatly next to the *tefillin*.

This story may or may not be true. The lesson in any case is real and only slightly humorous. How often do we behave dishonestly to achieve our selfish goals?

BE HONEST, BE
STRAIGHT, HASHEM'S
ON YOUR SIDE;

don't you believe that

He can provide?

חותמו של הקב"ה אמת (שבת נה.)

פרשת ויקרא
Real Freedom

In this week's *parshah,* we are introduced to the *Korban Minchah* – the "meal" offering. The *Korban Minchah* usually contained flour, oil and some water, but the Torah forbids us to let it rise so that it should not become *chametz*. Rabbeinu Bacheye gives a logical explanation for this year-round restriction, based upon a Gemara.

The Gemara (*Brachos* 17a) tells us that at the end of his *davening*, Rav Alexandrie would implore Hashem to understand that the will of each Jew is really to do *His* will. It is, however, the "yeast in the dough" – שְׂאוֹר שֶׁבְּעִיסָה that interferes. Rashi explains that he was referring to the *yetzer hara*. The evil inclination is compared to leaven, which causes the dough to rise and become *chametz*. So too, the *yetzer hara* will "raise" a person's ego, producing haughtiness and providing a false license to sin (*Sefer Hachinuch*). The function of most *korbanos* is to help atone for sin. Therefore, it stands to reason, explains Rabbeinu Bacheye, that *chametz*, which symbolizes the *yetzer hara*, has no place on the *Mizbei'ach*. *We are looking to rectify sin, not to exacerbate it.* With this understanding, we could perhaps appreciate why the prohibition against *chametz* is so extensive and severe on Pesach. The freedom which we celebrate on Pesach is the free-will which we exercise to be עַבְדֵי ה' (servants of Hashem), rather than to be slaves to Pharaoh. We are *not* celebrating the freedom to live *without* divine limits or to be enslaved to our own temptations. Thus the Torah demands that we not own, eat or benefit from *chametz* throughout Pesach. We are not to confuse real freedom with the masquerade of the *yetzer hara*. Thus *Chazal* declare, אֵין לְךָ בֶּן חוֹרִין אֶלָּא מִי שֶׁעוֹסֵק בַּתּוֹרָה – *The only free person is he who is busy with Torah*. Torah is the vehicle which Hashem has bestowed upon His people to escape the clutches of the *yetzer hara*. Only Torah can maintain us as a truly free people.

A parable is given of two leaves on a tree who were bemoaning their lot in life; anchored to a branch, "deprived of freedom." One day a strong wind blew one leaf off. As the falling leaf was happily "gaining his freedom," the remaining leaf jealously looked on. However, two days later, the tables were turned. The fallen leaf began to shrivel, while the leaf attached to the branch was robust with life.

עֵץ חַיִּים הִיא לַמַּחֲזִיקִים בָּהּ – Torah is a tree of life to those who grasp onto it.

What strategies work against your *yetzer hara*?

It was in the year 2010 that my dear father-in-law, Rabbi Eliyahu Meir Weinberger זצ"ל, returned his precious *neshamah* to its Maker. For most of his life, he taught small children in Toras Emes Kaminetz in Brooklyn, New York. He loved people, and he especially loved children. His beginnings were very difficult. He was raised in Vienna, Austria, and at the tender age of nine his father died of pneumonia. Four years later his mother was deported to Riga, where she was killed by the Nazis ימ"ש. His life was spared by the Kindertransport (children's train) in 1938, through the herculean efforts of Rabbi Dr. Solomon Schonfeld and Mr. Julius Steinfeld. This took him as a child of thirteen to Cardiff, South Wales, where he lived for four years before going to the famous Gateshead Yeshivah in England.

He would often tell us about his years in Cardiff. One particular episode depicts the freedom which he experienced, yet the self-control which he exhibited. In South Wales he went to public school where he learned English and other secular studies. In addition, he learned Torah with a *talmid chacham* by the name of Rabbi Rogosnitsky, of whom he was very fond. In the public school he was very well-liked and respected by his teachers. A certain non-Jewish teacher, Mr. Crowsther, invited my father-in-law to his home after school one day. It appeared that he wanted to show off his prized student to his friends. Once my father-in-law realized the purpose of this visit, he felt acutely embarrassed and self-conscious. He knew that his every act was being closely scrutinized. Mr. Crowsther then asked him to partake of the food which he had prepared for his guests. Although my father-in-law realized that he might be jeopardizing his good standing, he nevertheless responded, "I am sorry, I cannot eat anything. I am Jewish and this is not kosher."

The words that Mr. Crowsther then uttered stayed with my father-in-law for the rest of his life. He shared them with us, for he obviously realized their critical implication for his children. He said, "I did not know this, but had I known this and you would have eaten, I would have lost all my respect for you."

My father-in-law, even as a teenager, was a בֶּן חוֹרִין – choosing to be truly free to serve Hashem without bowing to external pressures. Throughout his life he was connected to our Torah – his tree of life.

יהי זכרו ברוך

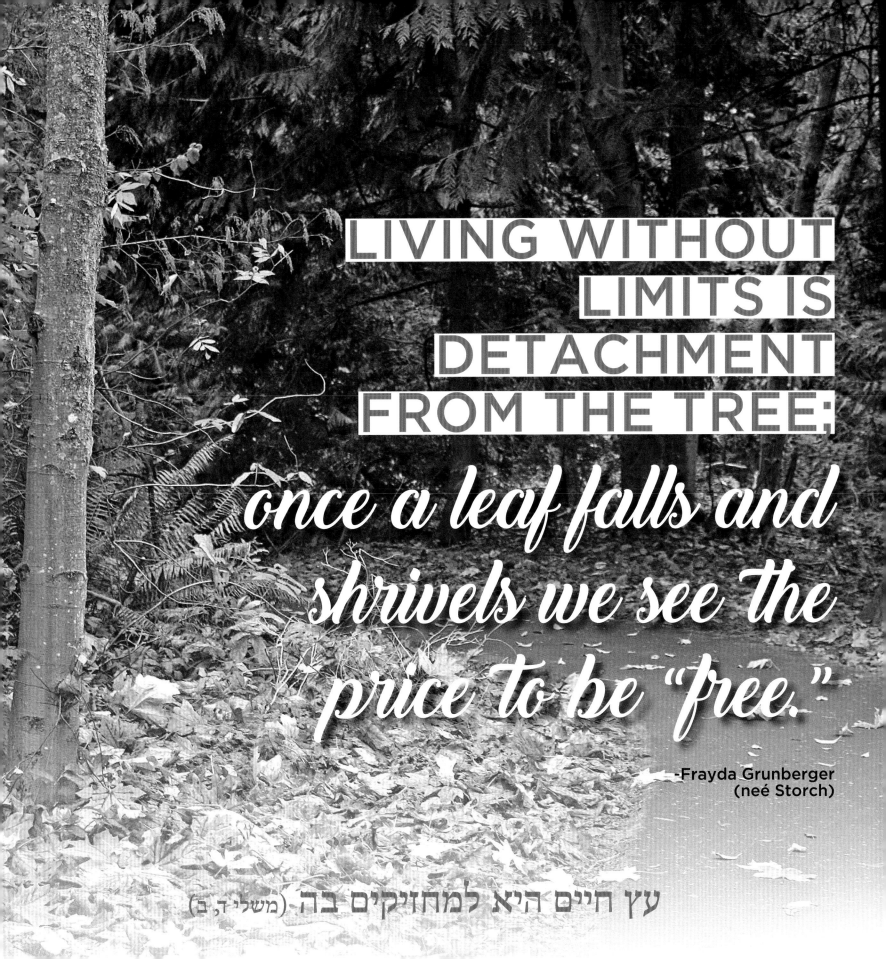

LIVING WITHOUT LIMITS IS DETACHMENT FROM THE TREE; once a leaf falls and shrivels we see the price to be "free."

-Frayda Grunberger
(neé Storch)

עץ חיים היא למחזיקים בה (משלי ג, ב)

Expressing Thanks

Among the *korbanos* that are mentioned in this week's *parshah* is the *Korban Todah*. This offering was brought by an individual who wished to express his thanks to Hashem for having been saved from an extraordinary danger. The Gemara in *Brachos* (54b) gives four examples: A person who recovered from an illness, an individual who was released from prison, someone who safely crossed the ocean, or a traveler who made it through the desert. Today, in place of this *korban*, we say in our *davening* "*Mizmor L'sodah*," the *tefillah* sung by the *levi'im* as the *Korban Todah* was brought in the Beis Hamikdash.

This *korban* was unique, explains Rav Shimon Schwab ז"ל, in that the *lachmei todah* (the breads of the accompanying *minchah* offering) consisted of both matzah *and* chametz. Rav Schwab explains that the matzah symbolizes salvation from grave danger, similar to that of *Yetzias Mitzrayim*. The *chametz*, "the everyday usual bread," represents the daily miracles we experience which we often take for granted.

The Netziv presents a classic and original explanation as to why the *Korban Todah*, with its forty "*lachmei todah*," had to be eaten before the next morning. Other private *shelamim* (peace offerings) were allowed to be eaten throughout the next day; why then was the time period for this *shelamim*, the *Korban Todah*, shortened? It would seem that eating the many loaves would require more, rather than less, time. He explains that in order to eat all the challos before the day ends, the person would be forced to invite additional friends to partake in the loaves of bread with him. *This gathering would enable him to publicize all his good fortune to the large assembled crowd.* This, explains the Netziv, is ultimately the purpose of the *Korban Todah*. With this, the Netziv continues to explain why we say in Hallel: (תהלים קטז, טז) לְךָ אֶזְבַּח זֶבַח תּוֹדָה – *To You I will sacrifice a thanksgiving-offering*, נֶגְדָה נָּא לְכָל עַמּוֹ – *in the presence of His* entire *people*.

A person who is truly grateful to Hashem will publicize his appreciation to as many people as possible.

Why is it hard at times to express thanks?

When a healthy child is born into a family, the happy shouts of "Mazel tov" resound throughout the home and throughout the community. But what happens when one's first child is a boy born with a rare condition? How does one prevent those happy cries of "Mazel tov" from becoming cries of disappointment, sorrow and shock? Such was the challenge when our grandson, Dovid, was born. The medical team at Sinai Hospital and then at Johns Hopkins Medical Center spent weeks and months trying to diagnose and treat this highly unusual case, in which Dovid grew no hair and had minimal body control. Although there was the regular *shalom zachar,* and the *pidyon haben* which took place in the hospital on the thirty-first day, the *bris* took place many months later.

As time progressed and Dovid came home from the hospital, it became evident that he was a very special boy who could only live through the natural and supernatural intervention of Hashem. This alone strengthened our children's *bitachon*, knowing that they were given an exceptional gift, with Hashem close by to guide them. A *seudas hoda'ah* (a meal of thanksgiving) was arranged when Dovid turned three, with the grateful participation of close friends, family and medical personnel.

As Dovid continued to grow, there were frequent emergencies in which he would turn blue, in desperate need of oxygen. *Baruch Hashem* there always "happened" to be a tank nearby, to restore his complexion, although urgent runs to the hospital were not uncommon.

In March of 2010 Dovid celebrated his bar mitzvah. This was a bar mitzvah like no other. The bar mitzvah boy did not read the Torah, he did not give a *pshetel*, nor did he feast from the delicious *seudah* prepared in his honor. Family and friends filled the catering hall on a weeknight to sing and speak the praises of Hashem. Dovid was smiling from ear to ear as his wheelchair swung around in every direction guided by children and adults dancing to lively music. Had Dovid been able to speak he would have said, "Thank you, Tatty and Mommy, for helping me reach this milestone and thank You, Hashem, for bringing me into such a loving and happy home." The theme of the evening is best summed up by Dovid Hamelech as he says in *Tehillim* (69:31), אֲהַלְלָה שֵׁם אֱלֹקִים בְּשִׁיר, וַאֲגַדְּלֶנּוּ בְתוֹדָה – *I shall praise the name of Hashem with song and I shall magnify it with thanks.*

Dovid returned his pure and precious *neshamah* to Hashem on Monday evening, ה' אדר שני תשע"ו (2016). Hundreds of people gathered together at the *levayah* to hear how Dovid was *mezakeh* (enabled) so many individuals, by helping them to fulfill *their* potential.

תהא נשמתו צרורה בצרור החיים

Appreciation felt but not said
IS LIKE A LETTER WRITTEN BUT NOT READ.

הא למדת שמפיית הטובה הוקשה לכפירה בעיקר (ירושלמי ברכות ג)

פרשת שמיני
The Main Thing

After detailing the animals, fish and birds which are or are not kosher, the *parshah* concludes, explaining the basis for this mitzvah: *For I am Hashem who elevated you from the land of Egypt.* Rashi explains that the purpose of *Yetzias Mitzrayim* was so that His people would accept His commandments. In the words of Rashi, *Had I elevated you from Egypt only so that you would not defile yourselves by consuming creeping creatures, it would have been enough.*

This statement is quite puzzling! How great is the sacrifice for a Jew not to eat ants, rodents or bugs? We naturally find them repulsive. Why then is Hashem satisfied (so to speak) with such a minimal commitment? The Ksav Sofer explains Rashi's point. Hashem wants His people not to ingest insects, not simply because they are disgusting, but rather because this is His will (רצון ה'). This is consistent with Rashi's quote at the end of *Parshas Kedoshim*: "Do not say 'I cannot stand pig meat'! Rather, you should say, 'I would love pig meat but what can I do, Hashem forbade it.'" Accordingly, our nation's greatness is shown, and we are thus elevated, when our sole motivation not to eat bugs is so that we not violate our Creator's will and not because we find them repugnant.

Following the רצון ה' throughout our daily routine – in and out of our homes – can be challenging at times. Rabbi Berel Wein recounts that in the beginning of his career he worked in the same office as Rabbi Alexander Rosenberg ז"ל, the founding head of the Kashrus Division of the OU (and the father of the late Dr. Naomi Baumgarten ע"ה). People would come with all kinds of elaborate (and sometimes shady) proposals to enhance their own status or that of the OU. Invariably, Rabbi Rosenberg's response would be the same four words: "*Und Vos Zugt G-tt?*" (And what does G-d say?)

The main thing in our lives is to keep those four words "front and center," parallel to Dovid Hamelech's four words: שויתי ה' לנגדי תמיד – *I always place Hashem before me.* If we can accomplish this we can guarantee that our internal "compasses" will more likely be calibrated correctly.

> **Your friend disregarded your need for help. What would *ratzon Hashem* dictate if the next day you had an opportunity to help her?**

It isn't always easy to decide which is the correct path to follow in life. It is for this reason that we have our עיני העדה ("eyes" of the congregation) – our *chachamim* who help us determine what is the רצון ה'. Such was the dilemma in which Rav Hirsch Diskind זצ"ל, Dean Emeritus of Bais Yaakov of Baltimore, found himself. It was in the early years of the school when there was only one other Jewish alternative for a girl in Baltimore. The other school had a bas mitzvah ceremony, at which time the girls would be "confirmed" upon reaching the age of twelve. One of the ladies involved in the school approached Rav Diskind and asked why Bais Yaakov could not do the same. Rav Diskind's immediate reaction was politely negative, saying that we do not celebrate bas mitzvahs. The woman, however, was not satisfied, and persisted. Knowing that this lady would respect and not challenge the decision of his illustrious father-in-law, Rav Yaakov Kamenetsky זצ"ל, Rav Diskind decided to speak to him. He was quite certain that Rav Yaakov would agree with him.

To the total amazement of Rav Diskind, Rav Yaakov felt that it was truly important to celebrate the occasion of a Jewish girl turning twelve. This was an important milestone in a girl's life. Rav Diskind then retorted to his father-in-law that if Bais Yaakov followed the lead of the other school, the next step would be to issue bas mitzvah certificates, just like the other school did. To the continued amazement of Rav Diskind, Rav Yaakov said that was absolutely an excellent idea. Rav Yaakov explained that numerous problems, relating to the writing of *gittin* (divorce), were surfacing when young ladies did not know their correct Hebrew or Jewish names. He felt that if an accurate certificate was issued when a girl became bas mitzvah, this problem would be alleviated.

The *gadol hador* clarified the רצון ה'. To this day, we at Bais Yaakov of Baltimore have a mother-daughter bas mitzvah dinner, at which time a certificate is issued to each girl with her correct Hebrew or Jewish name. Following the רצון ה' sends ripples which can be felt for generations to come.

The Main Thing is to keep the Main Thing,

THE MAIN THING!

(Heard from Rabbi Avraham Chaim Feuer)

שויתי ה' לנגדי תמיד (תהלים טז, ח)

Windows and Mirrors

The symptoms of נֶגַע צָרַעַת – the affliction of *tzara'as* – are carefully explained in our *parshah* this week. When it occurred on the body, it usually began as a white discoloration, which needed to be shown to the *kohen* for a diagnosis and for follow-up. *Tzara'as* was brought on by Hashem due to insensitivities that the *metzora* (the afflicted person) displayed toward another person. The Gemara says that the primary cause was *lashon hara* or *motzi shem ra* – falsely spreading a bad name.

(מְצוֹרָע is a contraction of those words: מוציא שם רע.)

The *metzora*, having abused the privilege of living harmoniously among people, forfeits this right and is sent outside the community until the *kohen* determines that he may begin the re-entry process.

If a *kohen* himself is afflicted, then he must show it to another *kohen*. He cannot self-diagnose his own *tzara'as*. In the words of the Mishnah כָּל הַנְּגָעִים אָדָם רוֹאֶה חוּץ מִנִּגְעֵי עַצְמוֹ (נגעים ב, ה). The rationale behind this is simple: No individual can be totally objective, and he will not be able to assess his own situation accurately. He will not be able to see his own "problem." In the same vein *Chazal* admonish us by saying, קְשׁוֹט עַצְמְךָ וְאַחַר כַּךְ קְשׁוֹט אֲחֵרִים – first correct yourself, and only then can you think of correcting others. It is obviously a great challenge to see our own faults.

The Chafetz Chaim (שמירת הלשון, חלק שני) goes so far as to say that if we would pay more attention to our own shortcomings, we would be less prone (or have less time) to find faults in others. We may even have an easier time "connecting" with others. In fact, the Chafetz Chaim explains why the *metzora* has to tear his clothing and why his hair remains uncut. This should humble him, so that he can repent and begin to see his own imperfections.

We refer to a person who has a personal involvement (or a bias) as one who has a נְגִיעָה, or as one who is נוֹגֵעַ בְּדָבָר. It is a form of נֶגַע (affliction) in which he cannot be objective. It is similar to a person who wears shaded lenses through which everything he sees is colored. When a person has a נְגִיעָה, self-analysis is just about impossible, and self-deception is just about inevitable.

The word נֶגַע (affliction) and עֹנֶג (pleasure) have the same letters. Rav Eliyahu Lopian זצ"ל says that it all depends on where we place the "ע." If our עין (eye) is placed first and foremost on ourselves, and we correct our own shortcomings, we will enjoy pleasure – עֹנֶג. If our own עין comes last, not being directed inward, we may experience נֶגַע – affliction – until we reposition our own critical eye inward, and correct our own faults.

How has a bias ever affected your ability to make a decision?

After my wife and I were married, our health insurance carrier was Blue Cross/Blue Shield. One day we received a check in the mail from them for $229.26. They explained that we had overpaid our premium by this amount and they were therefore returning the excess. Upon checking our records, we realized that indeed we had overpaid the premium, but only by $69.86. They sent us $159.40 too much. The question which we now entertained was what to do with the money. It seemed absurd to return this newly found money, especially in light of the fact that it was their mistake, and we clearly needed it more than Blue Cross/Blue Shield. For this multi-billion dollar insurance company, this money was pittance in their budget, and they certainly would not miss this money. Yet, something was gnawing at us, and we realized that we had a moral and halachic dilemma on our hands.

We decided to call our *rav*, Rav Shimon Schwab זצ"ל. After exchanging greetings, I explained the situation to him. I remember clearly the words I used when I asked the *she'eilah*, hoping for a favorable response: "Is there any reason why I can't keep the money since I did not lie, cheat or do anything dishonest?" Rav Schwab responded in a very soft and calm voice by asking, "Is the money coming to you?" I quickly answered no, and I repeated, "But I didn't lie, cheat or do anything dishonest." Again, he repeated, "Is the money coming to you?" I said, "No." He told me that we had an opportunity here to create a *kiddush Hashem* by returning the excess money with an explanation. He directed us to write a note saying that we, as Torah-observant Jews, are returning the money that was sent to us by mistake. We did so, and a few weeks later, we received a return letter thanking us for our honesty, as they realized that it was an error on their part.

In retrospect, it is clear that due to my bias (נְגִיעָה), it was impossible for me to see what was right. My desire to keep that money formulated the precise words with which I asked my *rav* the *she'eilah*. This episode, which took place many years ago, taught me the power of a נְגִיעָה, as well as the importance of not passing up an opportunity to make a *kiddush Hashem*.

*Check your window
to see with whom you
can connect;*

CHECK YOUR
MIRROR TO NOTE
WHOM YOU
SHOULD FIRST
CORRECT.

קשוט עצמך ואחר כך קשוט אחרים (בבא מציעא, קז:)

Finding the Light in the Tunnel

If we carefully study the topic of *nigei batim* (*tzara'as* which appears on one's house in Eretz Yisrael), we can discover the merciful "Hand" of Hashem.

The Torah tells us in this week's *parshah* that before the *kohen* comes to diagnose the deep green or deep red discoloration on the walls of one's home, the owner should remove his possessions. This is done in order to spare the homeowner the loss of property, which may result once the *kohen* declares the home, and consequently its contents, *tamei* – impure. This sensitivity may seem to be unjustified, since, according to the Gemara (*Erchin* 16) this plague is a punishment for the inhabitant's selfishness in not sharing his possessions with his neighbors. Perhaps he once excused himself by stating that he did not have what his neighbor requested, and now he is forced to show them what he truly owns. The *Yalkut Lekach Tov* explains, however, that this sympathy is truly consistent with Hashem's *middah* of *rachamim*. Hashem will demonstrate kindness even when He must mete out retribution, since Hashem is *rachamim b'din* (merciful in judgment).

This thread of kindness continues as we follow the development of this form of *tzara'as*. If, after the home is quarantined for seven days, the discoloration on the stones spreads, the owner must cut them out and reset them with new stone, mortar and plaster. If another week passes, and the *nega* (affliction) reappears, the entire house must be demolished. Where is the "silver lining" in this harsh judgment? Rashi explains (14:34) that when the Canaanim saw that the Jewish people would conquer the land, they hid their valuables in the walls of their houses. Now, "thanks" to this affliction, these treasures would be uncovered for the benefit of its new inhabitants.

Although *tzara'as* in any of its forms (on the flesh, clothing or home) is not found today, its lessons are forever. And although Hashem does not condone selfish behavior, His justice is tempered with mercy.

Whenever we go through difficult times, we must look to see the light, not at the *end* of the tunnel, but even *in* the tunnel.

Why is it so hard to see the light *inside* the tunnel?

There are certain people who are brought into this world, whose lives may be tragically brief, yet incredibly inspirational. Such was the life of Devora Butler ע"ה.

Devora was born in 1976 with an illness that was a medical mystery at that time. From birth her body did not function like the body of a regular infant, and she had a unique condition in that she was lacking tears. Later medical science would identify this Jewish genetic illness as Familial Dysautonomia, a disorder of the autonomic nervous system. Her parents, Rabbi and Mrs. Yale Butler, stopped at nothing, seeking the best medical care while securing the profound *brachos* of the illustrious Klausenberger Rebbe, Rav Yekusiel Yehudah Halberstam זצ"ל. He gave Devora two prophetic blessings which enriched the lives of the Butlers, and were a source of hope throughout the thirty-three years of Devora's life. Against all natural rhyme or medical reason, the Klausenberger Rebbe assured the parents not to worry, for Devora *would* develop tears. Additionally, the Rebbe assured the Butlers that one day they would walk her down to the *chuppah*.

Miraculously, Devora did indeed develop tears. It was said that when she would cry she would smile, recognizing the actualization of the Rebbe's first *brachah*, as she gained optimism that his second one would also materialize one day. Although Devora's life was a continuous medical challenge, she did not let her problems defeat her. Quite to the contrary, she wore her signature smile proudly, not focusing on herself; always seeing what she could do to help others. Amazingly, she rejoiced at the news that a certain test was being developed to test for carriers of FD, even though she realized full well that had such a screening been around earlier, she would possibly never have been born.

As her principal in high school in Los Angeles, I saw her as an inspiration to students and teachers alike. Despite her unsteady gait, she did not want to be treated differently, and certainly not pitied. She never complained and always responded to an inquiry of how she was feeling with a very deliberate, "*Baruch Hashem*." Those two words did not just roll off her tongue, but were seated deeply in her heart. This refrain became her life-long "theme song." She always responded with a very hearty "*Baruch Hashem*."

The climax of her life came in 2005 when she married Kenny Kamiel. He would refer to Devora as the Rebbe's *brachah*, and she would refer to him as her *brachah*. When they came to our home in Baltimore during *sheva brachos,* the happiness that radiated from both their faces was just about tangible.

Devora returned her precious *neshamah* to its Maker on Shabbos, Erev Pesach 2009. Throughout her life the merciful Hand of the Al-mighty was extended to her through the *rachamim* of His various messengers, including the Klausenberger Rebbe. Interestingly, at her *levayah* in Pittsburgh we were challenged to limit *our* tears (due to Chol Hamoed) for a young lady who defied the medical experts with *her* tears.

תהא נפשה צרורה בצרור החיים

Don't see the light at the end of the tunnel,

SEE THE LIGHT THROUGH THE TUNNEL.

-Mrs. Yehudis Hexter

גם כי אלך בגיא צלמות לא אירא רע כי אתה עמדי (תהלים כג, ד)

Just Be Humble

Our *sedra* begins with a lengthy exposition of the role of Aharon, the *kohen gadol*, on Yom Kippur. Because only Aharon was permitted to enter the inner sanctum of the Mishkan, Hashem tells Moshe to remind Aharon that the latter's two sons, Nadav and Avihu, died when they "drew near" (בקרבתם) to Hashem, without having been expressly commanded to do so (see *Parshas Shemini* 10:1). This implies that the sons of Aharon died because they entered an area that was forbidden to them. This reason, however, is not mentioned at all in *Parshas Shemini*. There the Torah simply states that they "brought near" (ויקרבו) a strange fire that Hashem had not commanded them to do. The Sifra relates a disagreement among the *Tanna'im* as to whether their death was caused by their "קרבתם," their drawing near, or by their הקרבה – what they brought near. Whatever the case may be, is there a way to reconcile these two explanations?

Rabbi Samson Raphael Hirsch זצ"ל posits that their "drawing near" before Hashem was an indication that they did not respect their boundaries. He writes, "They did not understand the loftiness of the Jewish ideal, and the lowliness of their own status. This overestimation of their own importance was the subjective aspect of their sin and this is what brought about their ruin." Their haughtiness (הקרבתם) gave them license to stumble in what, and in how, to bring (ויקרבו) their sacrifice.

This approach is supported by the Sifra here which states that the original *pasuk* hints to this reality. It shows that Nadav and Avihu did not consult with their father Aharon, they did not consult with their uncle Moshe, and they didn't even consult with each other. Herein lies their underlying sin – an attitude of arrogance which paved their path with poison and which ultimately led to their demise.

With this approach we gain a deeper understanding as to why this *parshah* is read in shul every Yom Kippur. Aside from its obvious appropriateness, it shows us the dangers of haughtiness and lets us derive its positive counterpart needed for *teshuvah*. This is the quality of humility. Internalizing this *middah* directs us to appreciate all the undeserving *brachos* which we enjoy and we realize that we can't afford to abuse or misuse that most precious gift. This is the gift called life.

Why is it most challenging to be humble?

Among the people who helped shape my life was my dear *rebbi* and *rosh yeshivah* in Rav Breuer's *beis midrash*, Rav Naftoli Friedler זצ"ל. Rav Friedler had learned under Rav Schneider and later on under Rav Eliyahu Dessler, in Gateshead, England, before coming to America. In my four years there I not only learned in his *shiur*, but I also saw how he carried himself with dignity and modesty. He loved learning, he loved teaching and he loved interacting with people. He would share his contagious smile with men, women and children of all ages. In 1972, he became *rosh yeshivah* in Ner Yisroel Toronto, where he remained for about twenty years, and he then moved to Monsey, New York, where he continued to learn and give *shiurim*.

Our relationship grew deeper in 1970, when he acted as our *shadchan*, introducing me to my wife. Rav Friedler hosted my late father-in-law as a *bachur* during the war years when he lived in England! He maintained a very close relationship with my in-laws throughout his life in America. I remember visiting my *rebbi* in Monsey toward the latter part of his life. We went to shul together, and I was amazed to see him sitting in the *back* of the shul. That was Rav Friedler – not seeking *kavod*. I once confided in him that I was upset that I had worked very hard on a project, but received no credit. Not only that, but someone else was credited for its success. He calmed me down, saying that a similar incident happened to him, adding that the *real* credit comes to the legitimate person in the *Olam Ha'emes*, where it really counts. He had no qualms sharing a personal issue with me or feelings that might lesson his status as "Rosh Yeshivah."

As he was getting older, he decided to purchase a plot to be buried in on Har Hamenuchos in Yerushalayim. Being the great *talmid chacham* that he was, he was "entitled" to be buried in the rabbinical section, *Chelkas Harabbanim*. His reaction was telling and typical, "*Ich bin a pashute Yid* – I'm a simple Jew." He didn't need that *kavod*. And so it was that on that tragic day, the 21st of Av 5757 (1997), my *rebbi* was buried on Har Hamenuchos with "simple" people. Little did he or the family know, that a few years previously Rebbetzin Elyashiv was buried in the same area.

Fast forward fifteen years, and on the 28th day of Tammuz 5772, Rav Yosef Shalom Elyashiv was *niftar* and buried next to his wife. No longer was my *rebbi* buried among "simple people." Now Rav Friedler had a *chashuve* neighbor, and the *kavod* that he fled his whole life, pursued him even after his passing.

Interestingly, Rebbetzin Friedler, who consistently avoided the limelight in her life, was buried next to her husband on the 6th of Av 5772. This was the final day of Rav Elyashiv's *shivah*. A crowd of people crowded around his *kever*, mixing with those who had come to give the *kavod acharon* to the Rebbetzin. The ways of Hashem are truly mysterious.

Lower yourself,
TO RAISE YOUR
SELF WORTH!

בכל מקום שאתה מוצא גדולתו של הקב"ה שם אתה מוצא
ענותנותו (מגילה לא.)

פרשת קדושים
A Divine Standard

Parshas Kedoshim contains one of the most quoted maxims in Jewish life, 'וְאָהַבְתָּ לְרֵעֲךָ כָּמוֹךָ אֲנִי ה – *You should love your fellow Jew as yourself; I am Hashem.* Rashi asserts that Rabbi Akiva maintained that this is a כְּלָל גָּדוֹל בַּתּוֹרָה – a fundamental rule of the Torah. How are we to love our friends as much as we do ourselves? Is this humanly possible? Secondly, Ramban asks, how does Rabbi Akiva say in the Gemara (*Bava Metzia* 62a) that if two people are traveling and there is only enough water for one of them to survive, the person in possession of the water should drink it, even at the expense of the other? The primary obligation is to himself: חַיֶּיךָ קוֹדְמִים – your life takes precedence! How can this be reconciled with the Torah's mandate to love our friend as ourselves? Ramban answers that the Torah's edict is not referring to life itself. Rather, Hashem expects that we desire for our friends the same level of *achievement* and success *as* we do for ourselves. Our hearts are to be wide open to our fellow Jews so that we speak positively of them, champion their honor, and value their money as we do our own. This is alluded to, says Ramban, in the word לְרֵעֲךָ – *to* your fellow Jew, as opposed to אֶת רֵעֲךָ. The Torah is referring to that which belongs *to* your friend – not your friend's life itself.

When a potential convert appeared before Hillel and asked to be taught the whole Torah on one foot, Hillel answered him with the Aramaic equivalent of our *pasuk, That which is hateful to you do not do to your friend. This is the whole Torah and the rest is commentary – go and learn it* (*Shabbos* 31a). Is this to imply that a Jew can override a Torah injunction if he forgoes *his* sensitivities – if it is *not* hateful to *him*? May a Jew speak *lashon hara* against his friend if he doesn't object to his friend doing the same against him? The answer is a resounding no. Hashem sets the standard of right and wrong, of our ethics and our morals. This is why our *pasuk* ends with the two words: 'אני ה – *I am Hashem.* In the words of Rabbi Samson Raphael Hirsch, these two words "clarify that these teachings have nothing to do with selfish considerations or expediency. They are ordained strictly as consequences of a true awareness of G-d."

Herein lies the source of an objective, Divine standard of ethics and morality. No individual can determine what is good or what is bad without employing the eternal Divine yardstick of our *Torah Hakedoshah.*

> **How have *you* overcome compromising an ethical Torah standard?**

In my earlier years of education, I had a student whose father, unfortunately, was very ill. Sadly, it was necessary to put him on life support by which a respirator enabled the patient to breathe. Without it he could not survive. After a few days, the girl approached me and said that the doctor wanted to "pull the plug," saying that her father could then end his life "in dignity." I told her that the doctor's mandate was to sustain life, and he was never given a license to terminate it. We believe in the sanctity of life (קְדוּשַׁת הַחַיִּים), and we do not have permission to determine what quality of life is worth living. There is nothing more "dignified" than following the will of life's Manufacturer. The patient remained on the respirator and, unfortunately, lived only a short while longer. I would like to believe that my brief talk affected the family's course of action.

On a much lighter note, I remember the anger I felt when one of my teachers in elementary school perpetrated an obvious wrong. This particular teacher (whose name I remember well) marked an "X" in her marking book each time a child misbehaved. After a few weeks of a child accumulating "X"s, either the parent or principal would be notified. My seat was right in front, next to the teacher's desk, affording me a "box seat" to all the teacher's transactions. On one particular afternoon this teacher lost her temper and started berating one of my friends. She immediately opened her roll book, and next to my friend's name, started to mark one "X" after the other until the entire line was full. She then called in the principal and showed him "all the X's" that my friend had ostensibly accumulated over the past few weeks. I was furious at this miscarriage of justice, which I quietly witnessed. Half a century has passed, and I still remember the indignation which I felt toward an authority figure who could be so untruthful.

Being honest and ethical is what Hashem expects from *all* of us, *all* the time.

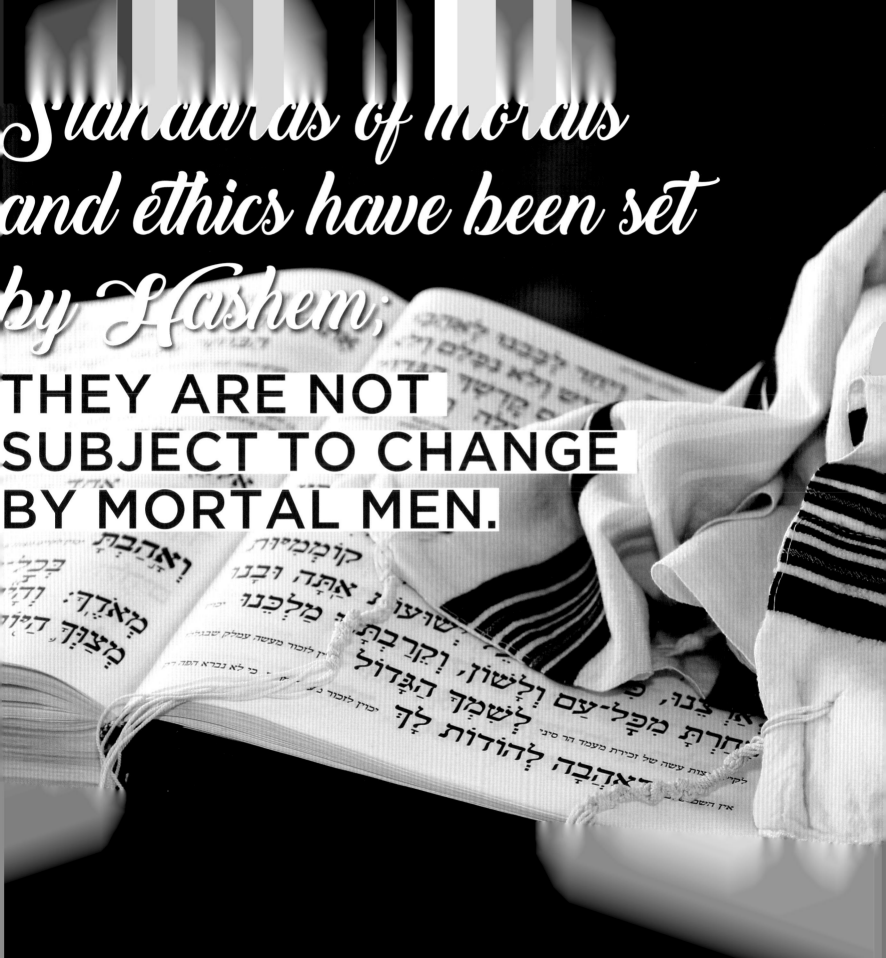

Standards of morals and ethics have been set by Hashem; **THEY ARE NOT SUBJECT TO CHANGE BY MORTAL MEN.**

A Priceless Gift

Our *sedra* details the counting of seven complete weeks, beginning from the second day of Pesach, when the *Korban Omer* was brought, until Shavuos. What could be the possible rationale behind this mitzvah? The *Sefer Hachinuch* writes that the *sefirah* (counting) reflects our enthusiasm and yearning to arrive at Shavuos – the time when we received the Torah. After all, the *Chinuch* continues, the entire purpose of *Yetzias Mitzrayim* was to receive this eternal, sacred gift.

But how is the Yom Tov of Shavuos to be actively celebrated? Regarding Pesach and Sukkos there is a disagreement between Rabi Eliezer and Rabi Yehoshua (*Pesachim* 68b) whether one needs to partake of a meal or whether can one just learn and *daven* all day. When it comes to Shavuos, however, they both agree that one also needs to eat and drink; there must be a physical component as well. The Gemara explains that this is so, since on Shavuos we received the Torah. The obvious question is: why does this compel us to have a tangible component? The reverse should really be true! Since this is the day we received the Torah, we should focus *exclusively* on our spirituality and ignore our physical needs.

Rav Eliyahu Lopian זצ"ל explains that the answer to this question sets us apart from all other people and philosophies. *Torah and mitzvos are to be used as a vehicle to elevate the physical, not to deny it.* Rav Lopian cites the Vilna Gaon who writes that Hashem created us with a *yetzer hara* (evil inclination) so that we have a desire to eat and drink and to satisfy our bodily urges. All these need to be *channeled* and *elevated* by the Jew. This is what *Chazal* mean when they say that we are to serve Hashem both with our *yetzer hatov* and with our *yetzer hara* (בכל לבבך – בשני יצרך).

Rav Shimon Schwab זצ"ל writes that the *Korban Omer* itself relays the same message. This *korban* consisted of barley, which the Gemara says is an animal food (מאכל בהמה). We begin the Omer count by specifically placing *this* on the *Mizbei'ach*, symbolizing our ability to elevate the mundane through *kedushah* (holiness).

On Shavuos we recognize the unparalleled, distinctive character of our *Torah Hakedoshah*. Through it we elevate our physical needs, transforming them into tools for spiritual growth.

What menial act can be raised through noble intentions?

Torah was, is and always will be the life blood of the Jewish people. From time immemorial our enemies have tried to deny this to us. I witnessed firsthand to what length our fellow Jews will go to preserve this most precious gift on a trip that we took from Los Angeles to Communist Russia in 1988. There I met a Yid who received permission to emigrate to Eretz Yisrael but was refused permission to take along his *sefarim*. Since these *sefarim* were printed in Russia, the regime considered them to be Soviet property. He wanted me to sneak them out of the country and then to mail them to him in Israel. I naively took his word that I, as an American citizen, would not be subject to any harsh punishment even if I would be caught; I would merely be sent home. Since he feared the KGB (Communist Secret Police), he asked me to meet him at night in a park opposite our hotel. I walked nervously into a dark area with the silhouette of a seated person highlighted by a single overhanging light. I sat next to him but he kept staring straight ahead when he mumbled, "Shalom." I responded the same. He didn't budge as he told me that inside the briefcase, which was between his legs, were the *sefarim*. He asked me to exit the park only after he left so that no covert KGB agent would associate the two of us. I followed these orders and I brought the briefcase to my hotel room. Upon examining the *sefarim*, I realized that some of them were over one hundred years old.

A few days later found our group in the St. Petersburg airport, loading our luggage onto the conveyor belt for exit inspection. Through this screening the Soviet regime hoped to prevent "contraband" from leaving the country. As our baggage passed through the x-ray machine, I prayed that the briefcase I was carrying would not be noticed. But it was. The operator ordered me to place it on the belt as she carefully scrutinized all the items on the screen. All of a sudden she stopped the conveyor belt and sounded the alarm. This immediately summoned two huge soldiers dressed in full military regalia. I froze with fear as I tried to remain innocently poised. They signaled me to empty the contents of my case, which I did. They thumbed through the *sefarim*, glanced at me and said, "Moscova?" I understood that they were accusing me of smuggling out Russian property. I quickly responded, "No, Los Angeles." In a stroke of Divine intervention, they looked at each other and walked away, allowing me to take home the *sefarim*. I can only imagine the joy that this Yid felt when he received his priceless *sefarim* a few weeks later, unaware of the trauma that I experienced.

Since we eat to live and we don't live to eat,

THE TORAH IS HERE TO ELEVATE EACH AND EVERY TREAT.

קדש את עצמך במותר לך (ספרי, ראה קד)

The Torah introduces the topic of *shemittah*, the Sabbatical year, by informing us that this mitzvah was given to Moshe by Hashem at Har Sinai. Rashi, as well as other *mefarshim*, are bothered by the specific reference here to Har Sinai, since all the mitzvos were given at Har Sinai.

What is the connection between *shemittah* and Har Sinai?

Rashi answers that the mitzvah of *shemittah* is to serve as a בנין אב – a general rule: Just as Hashem gave over the details of this mitzvah to Moshe at Har Sinai, so too, were all the other mitzvos given.

The question which remains unanswered, however, is: why was *shemittah* chosen as the model for all other mitzvos? The Chasam Sofer answers that *shemittah* is the surest example of a mitzvah given to us by Hashem, since no one can deny its Divine origin. Who else but the Creator Himself could guarantee that the harvest before the *shemittah* year would be so bountiful that it would be able to carry over for the following three years, until the next harvest? Thus, Hashem is saying that when one abandons his field in Eretz Yisrael once in seven years, this declaration of faith (כי לי כל הארץ – that the Land is Mine) does not go unnoticed.

The mitzvah of *shemittah* drives home our fundamental belief that Torah is מסיני. Our Torah is not only Hashem's plan for the world, but it is also the personal guide for each and every one of us. Our ancestors, realizing this, lived and died by the Torah. Throughout the millennia we have vigorously resisted any attempt by secular forces to reform Torah and to deny its Divine authorship.

Throughout each day we show our love for, and our acceptance of, the *dvar Hashem* contained in Torah. We place special value on our *sifrei kodesh*; we place them on top of other books, we kiss them and we stand up for those who teach them. The Gemara (*Makkos* 22b) bemoans the fact that some people are so foolish that "they stand for a *sefer Torah* but not for a *talmid chacham*." Through *kavod haTorah* we demonstrate and recognize the G-dliness of our Torah. Thus, the concept of a Supreme Authority and authority in general, is supported through the respect we show toward our Torah and toward our leaders.

> Why is the concept of "authority" frequently challenged in today's world?

Sometimes, our noblest efforts can fall short of our sacred goals. Here is a case in point. My first full-time teaching position was in the Ezra Academy of Queens. This was, and still is, a school for boys and girls who are not yet observant, but who show signs of wanting to become religious. I had many questions about the goals of the school and the best way to go about achieving them. At a Torah Umesorah convention in the mid 1970s, I was impressed by one speaker whom I did not know personally, Harav Yaakov Weinberg זצ"ל. I approached him privately, discussing numerous issues and challenges that I found in teaching. He responded saying that he could not give me any clear answers since he was not familiar with the school. He first wanted to come visit and see for himself before giving me any direction. I knew then that I had come to the right person, seeing the length that Rav Weinberg would go to before answering my questions.

A short time later, when Rav Weinberg came to New York, I picked him up from the airport and brought him to Richmond Hill, Queens, where the school was located. He wanted to observe some classes, speak directly to the students, and then he would meet the staff. After he observed some classes, I arranged for an assembly so that we could proceed with the next step. Of course, I "primed" the students so that they would act accordingly and give the proper respect. When Rav Weinberg walked into the room, all the students remembered to stand up respectfully. The first question the Rosh Hayeshivah asked the students was, "Why did you stand up?" To my bitter disappointment, one student raised his hand and said, "Because Rabbi Hexter told us to." Being thoroughly embarrassed, I smiled at Rav Weinberg, who went on to speak about the significance of Torah and the *dvar Hashem* which commands respect.

Before he left, he met with the staff and gave us tremendous *chizuk*, seeing firsthand what kind of students we were catering to. He continued to be an invaluable resource to me in my beginning years of *chinuch*.

Hashem gave us the Torah at Har Sinai; THROUGH SHEMITTAH, THIS TRUTH NO ONE CAN DENY.

אנכי

לא יהיה

לא תשא את

זכור את יום

כבד את אביך

לא תנאף

לא תגנב

לא תענה

לא תחמד

על ידי שמיטה נראה לעין כי התורה מן מהשמים ולא משה מעצמו אמרה (כתב סופר כה, א)

Holding on to the Spark

In the opening *pesukim* of *Parshas Bechukosai*, Hashem guarantees prosperity to His people when His commandments are obeyed: *The land will give its produce and the tree of the field will give its fruit* (26:4). In addition, the Torah states, וְנָתַתִּי שָׁלוֹם בָּאָרֶץ – *and shalom will reign in the land*. What kind of peace is the Torah alluding to? Is this referring to social harmony or peaceful coexistence with its warring neighbors?

Rav Moshe Feinstein זצ"ל deduces from Rashi that the *pasuk* is referring to peace *bein adam l'chaveiro*. Why else would it be necessary for Rashi, continues Rav Moshe, to comment that from here we learn that "*shalom* is equal to everything"? If this refers to the absence of war, why state the obvious? The Torah is thus stating that friendship and fairness will prevail once we, as His people, commit ourselves individually and collectively to His Torah and His mitzvos. Rabbeinu Bacheye concurs with Rashi as he cites the *pasuk* in *Yeshayah* (54:13) from which we learn that *talmidei chachamim* increase peace in the world.

Only through the study of Torah, and by deeply internalizing its lessons, will we be able to appreciate our individual blessings. This will then act as a shield to ward off the spears of jealousy and competition which attempt to drive a wedge between us and our friends. This is why we ask Hashem in *Shemoneh Esrei* to help us to be satisfied with His good – שַׂבְּעֵנוּ מִטּוּבֶךְ. When we focus on what we *have* rather than on what we *lack*, we are more apt to be content, rather than envious. The Ksav Sofer quotes the Ba'al Haflaah who interprets the main *pasuk* in *Ashrei* quite instructively: פּוֹתֵחַ אֶת יָדֶךָ וּמַשְׂבִּיעַ לְכָל חַי רָצוֹן – *Open Your hands (Hashem) and satisfy everyone with the* רצון *(will) to be able to be satisfied.*

The unfortunate reality is that our nature is as quick to welcome novelty as it is to get bored of it. We are not so different than the child who throws away yesterday's toy for today's trinket. Isn't this what we do when we discard last year's fashionable coat for the latest style? We become spoiled as we take our blessings for granted. When life then becomes "platitude" we sadly peek at our neighbor's wardrobe, home or car parked in his driveway. This attitude can even carry over to the myriad of natural miracles that keep us healthy. We feel entitled to them, not realizing how wondrous they are and how lucky we are. Perhaps we can ward off such an attitude by saying the *brachah* שעשה לי כל צרכי – *for providing me with all my needs*, thoughtfully and carefully, each and every morning of our lives.

How can we remain enthusiastic about all the *brachos* which we enjoy?

It was during 2002 when the Bais Yaakov Middle School in Baltimore was expanded and totally renovated. As the students walked into the building in September they couldn't believe their eyes. The entire building had been refitted with new windows, and six spacious new classrooms had been added, along with three computer labs, a state-of-the-art science lab, plus an expanded library and a spacious art studio. The gym was overhauled from floor to ceiling and the multi-purpose room was enlarged and freshly painted along with the rest of the school. One could hear the "wows" as the girls strolled down the halls with their mouths agape and their eyes feasting on their new treasures. But how long would this excitement continue? How long until the novelty would wear off? In an effort to forestall the inevitable we urged the girls to "let the 'wow' wax and not wane." But despite our noblest efforts, this beautiful facility has met the fate of similar creations, and now, years later, the sounds of "wow" have been silenced. Woe to the nature of man!

Although we are told never to make comparisons, sometimes doing so helps us realize how much we have to be grateful for. In 1965, while learning in Eretz Yisrael, I, with a few friends, decided to spend Shabbos in the Moroccan immigrant town of Azata. Rav Yisachar Meir זצ"ל was the *rosh yeshivah* there, and he was known to be very accommodating. When we came to *daven* Friday night, we were thoroughly embarrassed. Here we were in our hats and suits while the Moroccan immigrants sat with tattered pants, rags covering their bodies, and the traditional head coverings. We realized then how rich we really were.

And then there are the times when we may lose a gift temporarily, which makes us doubly appreciate when it is returned. Such was the case with the vision in my left eye. In the late 1990s, as I sat in my office after school, I realized that my vision was turning blurry. Upon the direction of my physician, I went to the Emergency Room where a resident doctor examined me. He scared me terribly as he explained some possible causes. Not feeling comfortable with his diagnosis, I asked to see my private ophthalmologist the next day. Dr. Michael Elman immediately diagnosed a torn retina, which he was able to repair in his office with laser surgery. How miraculous it was to have my vision restored! Unfortunately, only when faced with the possibility of such a tragic loss was I able to truly appreciate the blessing of sight.

Until this day, I try to pause and reflect when I say the *brachah* of פּוֹקֵחַ עִוְרִים – *He who opens the eyes of the blind*. Perhaps this will prevent one "wow" from waning.

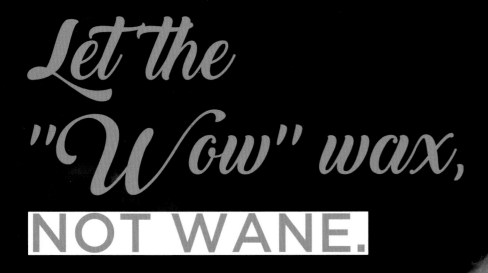

Let the "Wow" wax, NOT WANE.

כל הנשמה תהלל י-ה (תהלים קנ, א)

על כל נשימה ונשימה שאדם נושם צריך לקלס להקב"ה

(בראשית רבה יד, יא)

Everyone Counts

Each year *Parshas Bamidbar* is read on a Shabbos close to Shavuos. How can this *parshah* prepare us for the upcoming Yom Tov? Rav Moshe Feinstein זצ"ל explains that the census which our *sedra* details expresses a fundamental belief about the Jewish people. Each Jew who was counted was equal, regardless of his stature or accomplishments in life. This counting is thus the ultimate equalizer. No one can say (through misplaced modesty) that he is too low or too ignorant, and that he doesn't count. He is counted as one, on par with any Torah scholar. *Torah is accessible to everyone*. Thus the portion of the *pekudim* (counting) stresses the importance of each Jew, regardless of what he has or has not accomplished in the past. There is still time for him to realize his potential and to become great. To support this concept, Rav Moshe points out that the term used for counting Bnei Yisrael is שְׂאוּ, which literally means "lift." This word is used to indicate that this census is to lift the spirit of each individual, as he realizes that he is important and has a part in Hashem's Torah.

Chazal say, אֵין הקב"ה בָּא בִטְרוּנְיָא עִם הַבְּרִיּוֹת – *Hashem does not deal cruelly with people*. He only wants us to reach our personal potential, and does not demand more. It is therefore not surprising that the Gemara (*Bava Basra* 10b) relates how Rav Yosef, the son of Rav Yehoshua, slipped into a comatose state and "visited" the *Olam Ha'emes* (the World-to-Come). Upon awakening, he said that "upstairs" he saw an upside-down world: עֶלְיוֹנִים לְמַטָּה – there were those who were uppermost in this world and who were insignificant up there and תַּחְתּוֹנִים לְמַעְלָה – there were those who were lowly down here, and who were important in that world. In *this* world people are given prominence due to their *relative* accomplishments compared to everyone else. In the World Beyond, people earn distinction depending on the degree of their innate, *absolute* potential, which they have realized in this world.

We say in the *davening* of Shabbos and Yom Tov, קַדְּשֵׁנוּ בְּמִצְוֹתֶיךָ וְתֵן חֶלְקֵנוּ בְּתוֹרָתֶךָ – *Sanctify us with Your mitzvos and give us our portion in Your Torah*. The *Eitz Yosef* on the siddur explains that we are asking Hashem to help us access *our* individual spiritual potential; *our* portion in Torah. If we are granted this, our lives will be replete with growth, as we realize that in Hashem's eyes we count.

What are you doing to maximize your potential?

It was the summer of 1955 and once again Mr. and Mrs. Lou Herrmann were vacationing in the Luxor Manor Hotel in Ellenville, New York; gateway to the Catskills. As was his normal routine, Lou worked in New York City during the week and would drive up Thursday evening with two of his friends. When they left the city on this particular Thursday, the sky was clear and they were unaware of a bad storm approaching from the north. After driving for two hours and arriving close to their destination, it was raining heavily with the prediction of serious flooding. The car they were driving stalled by a small bridge which passed over a now raging stream. They decided to exit, and go to a nearby gas station to seek help. It was late, and no assistance was available, so the men called their wives, notifying them that they would walk the four miles to the hotel. Just as they were crossing the small bridge, a strong gush of water swept over the bridge, carrying away the three pedestrians. One friend's life was spared as he was miraculously tossed to safety, but tragically a second friend disappeared and drowned. Meanwhile, Lou was being swept downstream, stretching out his arms in an effort to grab onto something which would secure his life. Providence supplied a branch, and as he was literally holding on for dear life, he screamed for help. Lou, who at this point was not yet a fully observant Jew, prayed for help and asked Hashem to spare his life in exchange for a greater Jewish commitment. Finally, after two hours, a number of men made it to the site. As the water was raging they tried to make a human chain to rescue Lou, but they were unsuccessful. Finally, with the use of a car chain, Lou was able to shackle one end to himself and was pulled to safety. He was taken to the local hospital and treated for shock and minor wounds, and released on Sunday.

Realizing the Hand of Hashem, Lou kept his end of the deal. He began putting on *tefillin* from that point onward, and eventually became fully *shomer Shabbos*. Thanks to the selfless efforts of his dearest friend, Mr. Leo Hexter (my late father), he and his wife Lottie have children, grandchildren and great-grandchildren who are fully committed to Torah and mitzvos.

I was a child when this event occurred, and I vaguely recalled the accident. Years later, I called Mr. Herrmann and asked him to fill me in on all the details. Little did I know that he would pass away a few short months after this at the age of ninety-one. He was a close and cherished friend of our family, who, despite a late start, strove to maximize his spiritual potential. He was beloved by everyone who knew him.

יְהִי זִכְרוֹ בָּרוּךְ

ALWAYS REMEMBER:

You may be the only sefer Torah a stranger ever reads.

ואהבת את ה' אלקיך (דברים ה, ו)

שיהא שם שמים מתאהב על ידך... מה הבריות אומרות עליו
אשרי אביו שלמדו תורה (יומא פו.)

פרשת נשא
For the Sake of Harmony

Over seventy-five *pesukim* in this week's *sedra* are devoted to the offerings which the *nesi'im* (leaders) of each *shevet* brought during the inauguration of the Mishkan. Since each tribe brought the same gifts, why was it necessary to repeat the same words twelve times? The Torah could have simply mentioned the offerings of one *shevet* followed by the words "and so was done by each *shevet*." Since the Torah does not waste any letters or words there must be a very important lesson to be learned here.

The Chafetz Chaim quotes the midrash saying that all the *shevatim* agreed to bring identical gifts so as to avoid any possibility of jealousy and envy. That possibility had already become reality years before, when Hevel brought a different *korban* than Kayin. Hashem welcomed the *shevatim's* sensitivity to conform to one standard so He enumerated each of their gifts separately. Through this, Hashem emphasized the need to forgo one's individual preference at times in order to promote harmony. We especially see the emphasis that Hashem places on *shalom*, through our *parshah's* discussion of the *ishah sotah*. Here a wife who is suspected of being unfaithful to her husband is required to drink a potion in which Hashem's name has been dissolved. Hashem thus overlooks His honor so as to determine the woman's possible innocence and thereby reinstate *shalom* in the home.

The Mishnah says that Hashem could not find a more suitable vessel for *brachah* than *shalom* – harmony. With peace comes *brachah*; without it, *brachah* eludes us. Rav Shimon Schwab זצ"ל explained the concept of *ayin hara* (an "evil" eye) in the following way. Hashem does not want any individual blessing to create ripples of jealousy among others. Thus, when a person says "*bli ayin hara*," whether regarding children, health or wealth, etc., he is asking that no one be jealous of his *brachah*. For if this happens, Hashem may discontinue His *brachah*.

In most Bais Yaakovs, uniforms are worn to enforce *tznius* requirements and to minimize competition in dress. Those who say that this detracts from their individuality, must realize that ultimately this is determined through their personality.

A *yeshivah bachur* once responded to someone who criticized his "black and white" style of dressing. He explained that this was only his exterior look, and it does *not* relate to his individuality. He said, "Do you think I hang up my individuality each time I go to bed at night?"

> When did you find a situation that "*shalom*" pushed aside other considerations?

There are times when *da'as Torah* requires that the halachah be followed even at the expense of *shalom*. And there are other situations, such as the one which follows, where harmony is the overriding consideration, pushing aside other concerns.

Jessica* was living in L.A. and came from a "modern" family. She applied to a "modern" seminary, as well as to a more traditional one. Although Jessica was more observant than her family, her parents did not mind her applying to the second seminary since they were sure that she would not be accepted. You can imagine the excitement on Jessica's face when she was accepted to both seminaries. This is when the "battle of wills" began. She wanted to go to the more traditional seminary and her parents were adamantly opposed to it. "To add fuel to the fire," the teachers with whom she conferred were split in their opinion. There were those who said that she should hold her ground, and there were others who said she should give in. The amount of tension and discord which this created in the home cannot be imagined.

I was somewhat ambivalent, and did not express my opinion either way. Around the same time, I was scheduled to travel with a group of students to Eretz Yisrael, and I was hoping to discuss the situation with a *gadol*. Once I arrived in Eretz Yisrael, I contacted my oldest son, who was learning in the Mir. He told me Rav Shlomo Zalman Auerbach's *davening* routine so that we were able to meet him on his way to Minchah and escort him from his home to shul. He greeted us in his usual friendly manner, and I presented the issue, explaining to him the bitter tug-of-war which was currently waging between the child and her parents. He thought for a moment and then said that the struggle was not כדאי (worthwhile) and she should therefore go to the seminary of her parents' choice. Weighing the pros and cons of each choice, Rav Shlomo Zalman זצ"ל apparently felt that, in this case the path of *shalom*, especially *shalom bayis*, had greater merit.

*Name has been changed

Welcome conformity for the sake of harmony;

EXPRESS INDIVIDUALITY BY DEVELOPING YOUR PERSONALITY.

לא מצא הקב"ה כלי מחזיק ברכה לישראל אלא השלום
(עוקצין ג, יא)

פרשת בהעלתך
Change?!

Our *parshah* opens with Hashem giving Moshe the commandment concerning the lighting of the Menorah by Aharon Hakohen. This directly follows the inauguration of the Mishkan in the previous *parshah*, which involved all the *shevatim* except Shevet Levi, of which Aharon was the head. Rashi explains that the mitzvah of lighting the Menorah gave comfort to Aharon, since he was not included in the Mishkan's inauguration. Moshe taught the details of this great mitzvah to his brother and then the Torah states that Aharon *did so... as Hashem had commanded Moshe*. What is the significance behind these words? Rashi says that these are words in praise of Aharon, for not changing (any detail) – לֹא שִׁנָּה. The Maharal in *Gur Aryeh* explains why this would earn special recognition for Aharon. The igniting of the Menorah required painstaking exactness, so that all the wicks were facing precisely toward the center branch. This was prescribed by the Torah, and Aharon did not relax this requirement for his own convenience. He did not make any changes.

The Maharal (at the end of *Parshas Tzav*) gives another explanation which can be applied here. Although Aharon did not hear this commandment directly from Hashem but from Moshe, he still did it with the same care, enthusiasm and happiness as if he had heard it directly from Hashem.

The two explanations really go hand in hand. Aharon Hakohen toiled to perform his exact *avodah* since he considered it as a direct commandment from Hashem. It is easy to change or to make improvements on another person's suggestions; it is quite another thing to tamper with the Divine Will.

The veracity of this can be borne out through a cursory look at the Reform Movement. Once the movement abandoned *shemiras hamitzvos*, it wasn't long in coming that it rejected the Divine Authorship of Torah to justify their actions.

Our Torah, however, is not bound by time and Hashem provided us with the halachic process to make changes when necessary. This is the process that was used to write down our *Torah Sheb'al Peh*, which otherwise would have been left an oral law. More recently, this process allowed Sarah Schenirer ה"ע to institutionalize Torah learning for women.

Pirkei Avos teaches us to "do His will as you would your own, that He may do your will as though it were His" (*Avos* 2:4). We should consider each mitzvah as if we heard it directly from Hashem and carefully fulfill it as the halachah prescribes.

> **Why is change dangerous, although sometimes necessary?**

Every bar mitzvah boy is excited to begin fulfilling the mitzvah of putting on *tefillin*. For me, however, there were some minor complications. I am a born lefty and I do practically everything with that hand except perhaps cutting food or paper; this I do better with my right hand. The halachah states that the *tefillin shel yad* are to be worn on the weaker arm. Which was I to consider my weaker arm? My father ה"ע went to ask our *rav*, the illustrious founder of the German *kehillah* in Washington Heights, Rabbi Dr. Joseph Breuer זצ"ל. Rav Breuer advised him to have me write my Hebrew name from then on with my right hand and then to put the *tefillin* on my left arm, like everyone else. It seemed that the Rav did not want me to appear different from most people. He probably assumed that once I began writing my Hebrew name with my right hand it would become natural, and I would then be considered ambidextrous. This would require me to put my *tefillin* on my left arm. I did this for ten years, but the writing of my Hebrew name with my right hand still seemed very unnatural.

I was about to get married, and I bought myself a new pair of *tefillin*. I wondered if I should continue wearing my *tefillin* on my left arm so I spoke to my *rosh yeshivah*, Rav Naftoli Friedler זצ"ל. He decided to "revisit" the *she'eilah* with Rav Breuer. Rav Breuer then told him that I should change and put my *tefillin* on my right arm, as do all traditional lefties. Here, "change" seemed to be the route to follow after it went through the correct halachic process.

As we discuss the subject of "change" I can't resist including the following incident, although I am not sure of its implications. I was driving with my four-year-old granddaughter in the car and she asked me when we would be arriving at our destination. I told her in ten minutes. Five minutes later, she asked me the same question again and I said, "In five minutes." She paused, thought for a second and then said, "Oh, Zaidy, you changed your mind."

Surrender yourself to the will of Hashem;

KEEP HIS MITZVOS AND DON'T TRY TO CHANGE THEM.

ויעש כן אהרן (ח, ג) להגיד שבחו של אהרן שלא שינה (רש"י)

Finding Kedushah

Moshe sends out twelve *meraglim* (spies) to survey the Land of Canaan – the land that Hashem promised to Bnei Yisrael. They return after forty days with a negative report that devastates and demoralizes the people. The spies say that the people are powerful, living in fortified cities, and the Land is one that devours its inhabitants. "We cannot ascend to that people, for it is too strong for us." The Torah then reports that the entire nation cried *that* night. What night was that? The Gemara (*Ta'anis* 29b) says that was the night of the ninth of Av, the date when both *Batei Mikdash* (Temples) were later destroyed. Hashem said, "Since you cried that night without cause, I will establish that night as a time of crying for generations to come."

The implication is that because the *meraglim* sinned, both *Batei Mikdash* were destroyed! How can we reconcile this with the Gemara (*Yuma* 9b) that says that the first Beis Hamikdash was destroyed because of *avodah zarah* (idol worship), *gilui arayos* (immorality) and *shefichas damim* (murder) and the second was destroyed due to *sinas chinam* (warrantless hatred)?

Rav Shimon Schwab זצ"ל examines the root cause of the *chet hameraglim* (the sin of the spies). The *meraglim*, he says, did not see the inherent *kedushah* of Eretz Yisrael. Since they only focused on the physical appearance, they did not recognize the *Shechinah* on Har Hamoriah – the place of *Akeidas Yitzchak*, nor did they feel the sanctity of the *Avos* (forefathers) buried in Me'aras Hamachpelah in Chevron. He bases this idea on a midrash in *Eichah*. There it says that the *pesukim* in *Eichah* follow the order of the *Aleph-Beis* except for the "ע" and "פ" which are reversed. The reason for this is because the spies put their *peh* (mouth) before their *ayin* (eyes) by saying (*peh*) that which their eyes (*ayin*) did not see. Rav Schwab explains this to mean that they did not look at Eretz Yisrael with "spiritual eyes." Had the *meraglim* grasped the Land's sanctity and holiness, all their fears would have dissipated and they would have encouraged their brethren to enthusiastically go up and take over the Land.

This then is the answer to our original question. The *immediate* cause for the *churban habatim* was as stated in the Gemara in *Yuma*. The *underlying* cause, however, was the same as that of the *meraglim* – they did not perceive the unique *kedushah* of Eretz Yisrael which in itself would have prevented them from sinning. When one is cognizant of the fact that he is in the King's palace, he is careful with every action that he does and each word that he utters.

What can we do to retain our sensitivity to *kedushah*?

Would anyone think of going to Eretz Yisrael today without going to *daven* by the Kosel Hamaaravi? This was not the case in 1965 when I learned in Yeshivas Kol Torah in Yerushalayim. Yerushalayim was then a divided city with two huge fortress-type walls dividing the city; one was in Jerusalem, Israel and the other one was in Jerusalem, Jordan. A massive area of no-man's land was between the walls. The Kosel was then in the hands of the Arabs, totally inaccessible to the Jews. Many *bnei hayeshivah* tried to get a glimpse of any part of the Kosel from a high vantage point but it was to no avail.

When I returned for a visit after the 1967 Six-Day War, Yerushalayim's geography totally changed. No longer was Yerushalayim a divided city, and a giant plaza had been built in front of the Kosel, with easy access for every Jew.

There is one scene etched into my mind which I will never forget. Although traffic is generally barred from the Kosel Plaza, I recall seeing an ambulance driving slowly toward the Kosel. I stopped what I was doing to follow the unusual sight. As it came within fifty feet of the Wall it turned around and proceeded backwards. It stopped, and the attendant opened the rear doors of the ambulance, taking out the gurney on which lay what appeared to be an elderly gentleman. The patient was placed flush against the Kosel and I saw him raise his shaky hand and place it against the Wall. He kept it there for several minutes. He was then returned to the ambulance, after which it drove off. My heart tried to translate that which my eyes had just seen. Was this the patient's last request? Maybe he had just arrived from abroad and demanded to be taken to the Kosel. What *tefillah* was on his lips? Although I never found out any answers, I always remember the image of this elderly gentleman who appreciated the *kedushah* that rested within this Wall.

It is interesting to note that Rav Schwab himself was exceedingly aware of that which was beyond physical appearance. Toward the end of his life, my wife and I visited him in his apartment in Washington Heights. I asked him if my wife could take a picture of me with the Rav. He was very accommodating, and then pointing to himself, said, "But you know that this is really not me."

Rav Schwab looked behind the scene. He realized that beyond his human appearance there was a *neshamah*, a piece of G-dliness.

KEDUSHAH
YOU CAN FEEL
when to
you it is real.

טהרה מביאה לידי קדושה (עבודה זרה כ:)

The Quaking of Envy

Korach conspires with Dasan and Aviram to undermine the authority of Moshe and Aharon. In his egoistic desire to achieve his selfish goals, Korach draws 250 leaders to his side, claiming that Moshe's latest appointment of his cousin Elitzafan as leader of Shevet Levi was unjust. He declares that the position rightfully belongs to him. This rebellion was as much an attack against Hashem as it was against Moshe and Aharon, since all assignments were ultimately determined by Hashem.

What really was the cause for Korach's dissension? What was the driving force that could explain Korach's divisive behavior toward Moshe and Aharon? It was the ugly *middah* of *kinah* – jealousy! Korach veiled his envy, however, under a cloak of piety; as a champion of the masses: "The entire assembly – all of them are holy… why do you exalt yourself above the congregation of Hashem?"

To understand Korach's downfall is to understand the power of jealousy. Shlomo Hamelech says in *Mishlei* (14:30), *A tranquil heart is the life of the flesh but envy is the rot of the bones.* Jealousy creates an untruth within the psyche of a person, destroying his personal sense of mission and purpose. Hashem gives each person the tools *he* needs to accomplish *his* goals. The belief in *hashgachah pratis* dictates that each individual is personally taken care of by Hashem. *A person's total situation, including his resources and his personal challenges, is what he needs to fulfill his purpose in life.* Thus jealousy has no place. This would be as absurd as a diamond cutter coveting the lumberjack's powerful saw. The former could not do his job with the tools of the latter! This is what *Pirkei Avos* (4:28) means when it says, *Envy, lust and thirst for honor remove a person from the world.* These vices deter an individual from seeing *his* special mission in this world. Perhaps this is why Korach's household was banished from this world in such a horrific manner. The earth opened up its mouth and dramatically removed them *from* this world, since they did not recognize what their exclusive purposes were *in* this world.

Rav Nison Alpert זצ"ל suggests that Korach's terrifying demise exposed his deception. Korach presented himself as a spokesman *for* the people and *of* the people. Yet he was swallowed up alive, *apart from* the living and *apart from* the dead.

What strategies do you use to control envy?

While living in Los Angeles for sixteen years, we experienced numerous earthquakes. Even slight tremors can send fear and dread down anyone's spine. When the earth quakes underneath you, there is a feeling of helplessness. Initially no one knows its ultimate duration, and the possible destruction which it may cause.

One earthquake which I will never forget occurred on January 17, 1994, at 4:30 a.m. Our furniture started to shake and we felt as if we were riding on a train. The rolling motion continued to get stronger and stronger each second, and after about forty seconds (which seemed like an eternity) it came to a gradual halt. We left our home with our children, fearing that the initial movement might have weakened the structure of our house, and feared its possible collapse. Car alarms were blaring, caused by the shaking of the earth, and fire trucks were racing up and down the street checking for personal injury or property damage. The most serious damage in our neighborhood was the collapse of a highway and the toppling of numerous chimneys.

School was closed for a number of days in order to put the city "back in order." When school resumed, I heard a most incredible and inspiring story. A girl who "coincidentally" was away from her home on the evening of January 17th returned to her room after the quake to find a frightening sight. She saw that a window had shattered in her room, and glass "daggers" were imbedded in her mattress. Due to the quake, the window had fractured, hurling its pieces through the room and driving them into her mattress where she would have normally been sleeping. *Baruch Hashem!*

On a lighter note, I remember driving to school one day and stopping by a traffic light alongside two other cars. My car suddenly started to shake, and assuming that it was an engine problem, I popped the hood and inspected it. At the same time, the drivers next to me were doing the same thing until one observant fellow yelled out, "Earthquake!" and we quickly returned to our cars.

According to Ramban, Korach experienced an extraordinary earthquake, one which swallowed up his entire household and seamlessly closed up again. Although we don't see this today, earthquakes continue to send the message that Hashem is in control.

The seeds of envy
and jealousy

BEAR FRUITS
OF A FALSE
REALITY.

הקנא והתאוה והכבוד מוציאין את האדם מן העולם (אבות ד, כח)

Living a Double Standard

In the opening *pesukim* of our *sedra* we learn about the *parah adumah* – the Red Cow, which was used for spiritual purification. The *parah adumah* was taken outside the camp, *shechted* and burned. On the ash was placed cedarwood, hyssop leaves and crimson thread, after which they were gathered and preserved. When a person became *tamei* (impure) through exposure to a human corpse, these ashes were used as part of the purification process. They were placed into a vessel of fresh water and sprinkled onto the "contaminated" person on the third and seventh day. After immersion in a *mikvah* he was declared *tahor*, pure.

This mitzvah, which is the classic *chok*, Divine Decree, is a total paradox! These same ashes which were used to purify others, contaminated the people who prepared them (מטמא את הטהורים ומטהר את הטמאים). Thus Shlomo Hamelech refers to his inability to understand this mitzvah when he says, *I said I would be wise but it is far from me (Mishlei 7:23).*

The overriding question, however, is why the Torah introduces this *parshah* with the words זאת חקת התורה – *This is the decree of the Torah*. It would have been more precise to write זאת חקת פרה אדומה – this is the decree of the *parah adumah*. Rav Moshe Feinstein זצ"ל answers that *the paradox of the parah adumah is really the paradox of Torah life itself.* In one situation a particular character trait (*middah*) is beneficial, whereas the same *middah* in another situation, is detrimental. For example, *kavod* – honor, which is a virtue to exercise when dealing with others, is a vice when one demands it for himself. So too with the *middah* of generosity. We are to be generous with our own money, but stingy with the next person's finances; we cannot take a penny away from him. In the same vein, our own standard of *bitachon* (trust) should minimize *our* need for *hishtadlus* (effort), but this cannot be applied as an excuse not to lend a friend money. Thus the Torah expects a Jew to live a life of a *double standard* – one which encourages personal growth, yet another which is sensitive to the needs of others.

This then is the lesson of the *parah adumah*. Something which can be a source of "contamination" to one person, may be a source of "purification" when applied to someone else.

To what other *middah* can you apply a "double standard"?

Our daughter, Tzipora Appelbaum, is a shaitel macher in Kensington (Brooklyn, New York). She has a very diverse clientele, ranging from young newlyweds to older "bubbies." She attracts women who respect not only her expertise and professional work, but also her friendliness, honesty and calm disposition. Although she has a very busy household, she somehow manages to give all her children the time they need, while generously designating time for her customers.

A rather "hair raising" incident occurred some years ago. The *middos* that this episode brought out were not those which anyone would normally expect.

The mother of one of Tzipora's clients had come from out-of-town to attend a *chasunah* that evening in Brooklyn. In the afternoon, the customer came over with her mother's sheitel, asking Tzipora if she could fix it up. Tzipora, never wanting to say no, accommodated her, and asked that she return in two hours. Tzipora then put the sheitel down in her work room. Unbeknownst to Tzipora, her two-and-a-half-year-old son entered the room a few minutes later, got hold of a pair of scissors, and started to do his own "reshaping." When Tzipora later entered the room, her mouth dropped. What now? How could she have betrayed the trust of her loyal customer? What was the mother now going to wear? She felt terrible. She felt guilty of negligence and made up her mind to replace the sheitel, no matter what the cost may be. But what about the *chasunah* tonight? She picked up the phone to call her friend, expecting the worst. The response Tzipora received was quite to the contrary. "Don't worry, Mrs. Appelbaum, my mother will wear one of *my* sheitels tonight." Tzipora could not believe her ears! Was she talking to a *malach* or to a human being? Still feeling terrible, Tzipora worked for the next few hours and tried to "recoup" the sheitel. As the evening wore on she noticed that there was a message on her answering machine. It was the mother herself: "Don't let this cause you any *agmas nefesh* (aggravation). It's just a sheitel. You should only have *nachas* from your *kinderlach*." (This message was so inspiring to Tzipora that she kept it on her machine.) Tzipora fixed up the sheitel as best she could, and returned it to "Mrs. Malach," who refused to take any money for the damaged sheitel.

How paradoxical! Instead of the "victim" exacting retribution, she *defended* the "perpetrator." Instead of the guilty party rationalizing her actions, she *offered* to pay damages. The inner strength of both people is reflected in their ability to apply an exemplary *middah* during a most challenging experience.

מי כעמך ישראל!

Living a double standard is really okay

WHEN THE MIDDOS ARE APPLIED IN THE PROPER WAY.

איזהו מכובד? המכבד את הבריות (אבות ה, א)

Just Take the First Step

King Balak, the leader of Moav, was fearful of Bnei Yisrael as they advanced toward his country. Balak sent emissaries to the gentile Navi, Bilam, asking him to come with them to curse Bnei Yisrael. If a curse could be effected, then Balak would be able to defeat Bnei Yisrael in battle. After conferring with Hashem, Bilam tells them that he cannot go with them (עִמָּהֶם). Balak, however, does not give up and tries to feed Bilam's ego by sending more prestigious messengers than the previous ones. This time Hashem tells Bilam that since they came "to call for him," he can go with them (אִתָּם), with the stipulation that he only speaks the words that Hashem tells him to. All the *mefarshim* ask: Did Hashem change His mind? Furthermore, if Hashem did indeed concede to Bilam, why does the Torah say afterward that Hashem was angry that Bilam went? Hashem said that he could go!

Ramban answers that Hashem *did not* waver. Hashem consistently forbade Bilam to go with the emissaries *to curse Bnei Yisrael.* When Hashem spoke to Bilam the second time saying that he could go, it was with the understanding that he would not curse Klal Yisrael. Hashem got angry at Bilam for not articulating this stipulation to the messengers. A *chillul Hashem* was created for they thought that the G-d of the Jews had now consented to have His people cursed.

The Vilna Gaon supports this explanation by pointing out the difference between the words (עִם) עִמָּהֶם and (אֶת) אִתָּם. The former implies with the *same* intention, as opposed to the latter which implies with a *different* intention. Thus Hashem initially told Bilam that he could *not* go עִמָּהֶם – with the same intention to curse Klal Yisrael. Later, when Hashem allowed Bilam to go along, for a *different* purpose, the term used is אִתָּם.

One may challenge the Gaon's distinction between עם and אֶת, since the *malach* who appeared to Bilam later on said to him: לך עם האנשים, *go with the people*, with the *same* intention (to curse Klal Yisrael). The Gaon explains that this is exactly how *Chazal* learn from this *pasuk* that בדרך שאדם רוצה לילך בה מוליכין אותו – Hashem guides a person along the way that *he* chooses to go. Since Bilam wanted to curse Bnei Yisrael, Hashem accommodated that desire.

Why does Hashem allow people to choose the wrong path?

It is especially in the field of *kiruv* (outreach) where we see how Hashem guides those Jews who take a step to become *frum*. Being that Los Angeles is only 120 miles north of the Mexican border, some students of YULA had an unusual opportunity to spend a Shabbos with a tiny Jewish community just south of the border.

Tijuana, Mexico, is not a town teeming with Jewish life, yet the rabbi there was interested in bringing some youthful enthusiasm to inspire his congregants. The rabbi had recently arrived from Eretz Yisrael through the Jewish Agency and was disappointed with the lack of religious commitment which he quickly discovered. When he arrived, there was no *mechitzah* in the shul, so he naturally put one up. The next day he saw that the *mechitzah* had been taken down. He put it up again but that *mechitzah* was met with the same fate. He decided to commission a mason (with his own money) to build a brick wall which the congregants could no longer "play" with. By asking us to spend Shabbos with him it seems that the rabbi now decided to choose the path of inspiration rather than confrontation.

In preparation for this Shabbaton, the rabbi asked if I could speak to his congregation on Shabbos. I told him that I knew no Spanish. He told me that I should do the best I could. I agreed and wrote a speech in English which I presented to one of our Spanish-speaking mothers, who translated it into Spanish and who then recorded it onto a tape. On the two-and-a-half-hour bus ride to Tijuana, I listened to this tape over and again until I memorized it so that I could mimic it like a parrot, come Shabbos morning.

When we arrived on Erev Shabbos with our own food, we took up residence in a local hotel and found the tiny Jewish Community Center. We ate there, *davened* in the shul, and when I spoke there Shabbos morning, the congregants had a good laugh. Both my family and another family who came down with us from Los Angeles interacted with our new friends throughout Shabbos. On Motza'ei Shabbos our hosts hired a three-piece Mariachi band to complement our *melaveh malkah.*

The experience was very positive, although we don't know who gained more, the student participants or the adult recipients. One thing for sure, the Jews of Tijuana felt the pleasure of a youthful Orthodox presence which they never had experienced before.

However **YOU** *decide,*

**HASHEM WILL
BE YOUR
GUIDE.**

בדרך שאדם רוצה לילך בה מוליכין אותו (מכות י:)

True Shalom

Pinchas is rewarded by Hashem for killing Zimri, the Nasi, and Kozbi, the Midianite woman, after their public display of immorality. His reward is בריתי שלום – *My covenant of peace*. Why is an act of *killing* rewarded with a promise of *peace*? Isn't killing the antithesis of peace? Rabbi Samson Raphael Hirsch זצ"ל answers most succinctly: "There can be true peace among men only if they are at peace with G-d!" True *shalom* had been restored once Hashem's ire against His people had ceased. This was evidenced by the fact that the plague which took the lives of 24,000 people had stopped.

The word שלום in our *parshah* contains a broken *vav* (ו' קטיעה). This teaches us, continues Rav Hirsch, that for "completeness" (שלמות) to be established, it may be necessary to break the illusionary peace. Hence the broken *vav*.

Although *shalom* is one of the greatest qualities which we as a people aspire to attain, it has its limits. In 1954 a proclamation of the *gedolei Yisrael* forbade Orthodox congregations from joining the Synagogue Council of America, since it was composed of Reform and Conservative organizations. Rabbi Yosef Ber Soloveitchik זצ"ל explained that Jewish unity is based upon the concept of an עדה (a congregation), which comes from the word עדות (testimony). A Jewish community is only united when its members believe in the עדות that Torah is משמים – from Hashem. The Reform and Conservative movements do not accept this basic tenet of Judaism, and therefore cannot be part of a united עדה. *The pursuit of harmony did not justify uniting fundamentally disparate parts.*

The above attitude stands in stark contrast to Shlomo Hamelech's maxim, דרכיה דרכי נועם – *Her (Torah's) ways are ways of pleasantness!* As a rule, we are to foster friendly relationships, even when it may be necessary to abandon another virtue. For example, we may need to change the truth at times, in order to avoid a quarrel. So too, we can heal and promote the welfare of gentiles as we do with our fellow Jews, in order to promote harmonious relationships. The question of when one is to *pursue* peace, or when one is to *sacrifice* peace, is always a most challenging one. It requires great deliberation, for a mistake either way can be very detrimental.

When did you abandon your "wants" in order to promote *shalom*?

It is often difficult to determine when peace and harmony should be the overriding consideration. In 1993, I had the opportunity to serve as rabbi of the Young Israel of Los Angeles, whose congregants consisted primarily of people who had settled on the West Coast after the war. They were friendly and respectful, wanting to hold on to their particular *minhagim*.

There was one questionable *minhag* which they wanted to reinstate. Until recent years they did not *duchen* when Yom Tov fell out on Shabbos. Rabbi Tzvi Teichman, who preceded me, changed that to the more acceptable practice, which is to *duchen*. They now wanted to go back to the original *minhag* not to *duchen* on Shabbos which fell on Yom Tov. Was this a situation where I should "put my foot down" or should I "give in"? I called my *rosh yeshivah*, Rav Naftoli Friedler זצ"ל, to ask his advice. He told me that I should certainly try to maintain the practice of *duchenen*. However, I should only do this if it would not cause any *machlokes* – bickering or fighting. He felt that this issue was not worth an argument. Fortunately, I was able to carry out my *rebbi's* mandate, and they agreed, in principle, to *duchen* when Shabbos and Yom Tov coincide. What I learned from this experience was not so much the importance of *duchenen*, but the importance of factoring *shalom* into any halachic equation.

In a very different situation, there were three Iranian sisters in our school in L.A. who wanted to become *frum*. The problem was that their parents (who had only recently left Teheran) were committed to a "compromised Yiddishkeit." For example, they insisted that their children ride with them in a car on Shabbos. I advised the girls to do whatever they could to avoid *chillul Shabbos*. I remember one dramatic incident which occurred in our home, when we invited the three sisters to come for the *seudah* on Shabbos afternoon. Toward the end of the *seudah* there was a knock on the door, and facing me were two angry-looking parents. I invited them in and we began to talk. They were very bitter as they accused me of extremism – being like Khomeini, in my attempt to "brainwash" their children. I tried to get them to appreciate their daughters' noble goals, but it was to no avail. The girls' journey toward a life of *shemiras hamitzvos* was very shaky, but we are now happy to be able to enjoy the fruits of our labor.

As we can see, the question whether to follow the path of least resistance, or whether to persist, is always a most daunting one.

SHALOM MEANS PEACE AMONG MEN,

while being at peace with Hashem.

עושה שלום במרומיו הוא יעשה שלום עלינו (מתוך הסידור)

פרשת מטות
Confusing Priorities

Our *sedra* recounts how the tribes of Gad and Reuven approached Moshe, Elazar and the leaders of the people to make an unusual request. They asked if they could take their inheritance on the east bank of the Yarden; land which they had already conquered from Sichon and Og. They were attracted to this area since they had a great abundance of livestock and this land was an ארץ מקנה – a land rich for farm animals. Moshe was initially skeptical, since he felt that this action would demoralize the people: "Shall your brothers go out to battle (against Canaan) while you settle here?" Moshe only agreed after Bnei Gad and Bnei Reuven assured him that they would fight alongside their brothers, and only afterward would they return to the East Bank, having settled their families and cattle there.

The Midrash is critical of the actions of these two *shevatim*. In fact, it says that Gad and Reuven were the first of the *shevatim* to be sent into exile years later, because of this episode.

What exactly was their sin? The Midrash answers by saying that "they separated themselves from their brothers because they loved their money." Rashi takes note of the same point and says (32:17), "they valued their property more than their children." This is evidenced when they initially said that they would build pens for their flock, and only *afterward* build cities for their small children. Their priorities were skewed – עשו את העיקר טפל ואת הטפל עיקר – that which should have been primary, they made secondary and that which should have been secondary, they made primary.

Rav Aharon Kotler זצ"ל in *Mishnas Rebbi Aharon* learns two important lessons from this event. 1) When one's priorities are confused, success will elude him. This can be seen from the fact that ultimately the tribes of Gad and Reuven had to abandon their land first. 2) Every action, and every spoken word, is a reflection of the attitude which sits deep in one's heart. This clarifies the midrash which explains the following *pasuk* in *Koheles* (10:2): לב חכם לימינו זה משה – *the heart of the wise is to his right – this refers to Moshe*, ולב כסיל לשמאלו זה בני גד ובני ראובן *– and the heart of the foolish is to his left – this refers to Bnei Gad and Bnei Reuven.* Rav Aharon concludes that the more we strengthen our love of Torah, the more our every action and every word will reflect this priority.

How can we make sure that our priorities remain correct?

Renovation of the Bais Yaakov Middle School shifted into high gear during the 2002 school year and through the summer. In addition to remodeling the original building, eleven classrooms were added to accommodate the growing school population. At the same time, the entire landscape was being transformed, creating a new traffic pattern, by hauling and redistributing thousands of tons of earth throughout the property. A forest was planted where the previous driveway stood and a new hill was developed, as plows and heavy "earthmovers" worked steadily to create a new driveway for the campus.

As is common at every construction site, "No Trespassing" signs were conspicuously placed to deter strangers from roaming around the dangerous, rocky area. It was over the weekend that the Pikesville Fire Department responded to a 911 phone call from the middle school construction site. They dispatched their emergency rescue unit to try to save the life of a child who was rapidly sinking in a "quicksand-like" substance. It seems that a child from the neighborhood had wandered and became mired, and needed to be extricated safely. When the rescue unit arrived, they had to act quickly yet cautiously, so that they themselves would not become ensnared.

Baruch Hashem, the child was rescued unharmed. A deliriously happy mother grasped her child lovingly, hugging her non-stop. With tears in her eyes, she examined her child from head to toe, and astonishingly, in a matter-of-fact way, asked, "But where is her new watch?" Was this mother serious? How could she be so concerned with such trivia when her child's life had just been saved? Did she value the watch more than the life of her child? This mother's words exposed her as an ungrateful individual whose priorities were totally confused.

"*Life*" and "*Property*"
require protection

BUT "LIFE"
DEMANDS IMMEDIATE
ATTENTION.

עשו העיקר עיקר, והטפל טפל (רש"י לב, טז)

פרשת מסעי

The Master Plan

The first third of our *sedra* outlines the forty-two stops the Bnei Yisrael made as they traveled from Mitzrayim to Eretz Yisrael. Rashi explains that the Torah bothers to list this itinerary to teach us the compassion of Hashem for providing these encampments. No one should think that since it was decreed that the Jewish people had to wander in the wilderness for forty years, they therefore traveled aimlessly without respite. Upon studying the *pesukim* closely we see that the people did indeed stop and they frequently enjoyed long periods of rest.

Ramban cites Rambam from *Morah Nevuchim* who presents a different answer. The Torah records the entire route that our people traveled through the wilderness, highlighting the miraculous Hand of Hashem. Let the future generations know that Bnei Yisrael traveled through unpopulated and dangerous lands and only through Divine intervention did they survive their trek.

When introducing these travels, the Torah states that Moshe wrote (33:2), *their goings forth according to their journeys* (מוצאיהם למסעיהם) *and these were their journeys according to their goings forth* (מסעיהם למוצאיהם). What significance does this *pasuk* carry, and why is the expression reversed the second time? Rabbi Samson Raphael Hirsch זצ"ל says that this *pasuk* is describing the diverse motivations and the different attitudes which were present while traveling. The first segment characterizes *Hashem's* goal: to move *toward* their destination (למסעיהם): to take the next step in carrying out His Master Plan. The next part, however, is relating *Bnei Yisrael's* motive, to move on, to *leave* their present location (למוצאיהם). Wherever they stopped they were not content. Their main objective was to *decamp* – to *go forth* to any random station.

Rav Nison Alpert זצ"ל writes that these travels are a metaphor for man's journey through life. Perhaps we could add that although we make various "stops" and take different "turns" during our lifetime, they are driven by the overshadowing Hand of G-d. We plan and make decisions according to our own narrow thinking, but it ultimately unfolds following Hashem's Master Plan.

> **Why is it hard to remember that everything that happens is part of Hashem's plan?**

During the initial stages of the middle school renovation in 2001, trees were uprooted and vegetation destroyed in preparation for the construction of a new driveway. Giant machinery was brought in to handle this enormous task. When the young ladies of the middle school beheld what seemed to be random destruction, they panicked. They came rushing into the office, wanting to know why this wanton demolition was taking place. Very calmly and deliberately I brought them over to a wall on which was hanging a scheme of the builder's plan. After a few short minutes they were comforted in knowing that what was happening was not at all random, but part of a carefully orchestrated plan to expand and to improve the school.

So it is in life. Nothing happens by chance. Although we are not privy to the Divine plan of our lives, we know that there definitely is one which is guided by a merciful G-d. Every step and every turn in life's voyage is a step to actualize the Master Plan.

This lesson became very evident when the time had come for our family to leave Los Angeles, after living there for sixteen years. It was a beautiful day in April of 1994 when three incidents coincided, each pointing in the same direction. The first unmistakable "sign" occurred when a "For Sale" sign was posted by our landlord at the home which we were renting. On the same day we received two totally unrelated phone calls from two different sources. The callers informed us of two different job openings, both on the East Coast. One was in New York and the other was in Baltimore. After interviewing in both locations we moved to Baltimore, to become part of the Bais Yaakov family. These "coincidences" would have been enough to convince us that there is a Plan. Then a year later, tragedy struck. Our dear *mechutan*, Rabbi Yehuda Naftali Mandelbaum זצ"ל, suddenly died. The whole Baltimore community was taken by surprise as this beloved *rebbi*, husband, father and mentor was taken away in the prime of his life – without warning. We were glad to be here to lend whatever support we could to the children and to Mrs. Mandelbaum. We couldn't help but think that our move to Baltimore just a year earlier was part of the plan which enabled us to be with the family at this critical time.

It's all part of Hashem's plan,

YET WE MUST DO WHATEVER WE CAN.

בטח בה' ועשה טוב (תהלים לז, ג)

Hashem's Unconditional Love

Parshas Devarim begins with Moshe's words of rebuke to Klal Yisrael. Despite the failings of His people and His need to punish them, Hashem, as our Father, never abandons His children. Perhaps this gives us a better understanding why this *parshah* is read on the Shabbos before Tishah B'Av. His two *Batei Mikdash* were destroyed because of *our* shortcomings, yet Hashem waits patiently for our return.

The Gemara *in Kesubos* (66b) speaks of an unusual encounter between Rav Yochanan ben Zakai and the daughter of (the rich) Nakdimon ben Gurion, shortly after the destruction of the second Beis Hamikdash. Poverty was rampant and he saw her searching for food amidst the dung of animals. Rav Yochanan queries as to what happened to her father's wealth. She indicates that her father lost his wealth for not giving sufficient *tzedakah*. Rav Yochanan ben Zakai then states: "אשריכם ישראל – fortunate are you, the Jewish people. When you do His will, no nation can subjugate you. And when you don't do His will, you are given over, not only to a lowly nation, but to the animals of this lowly nation." The Lev Eliyahu quotes Rav Yehonasan Eibeshitz זצ"ל, who asks (as does the Maharsha): how is the statement "אשריכם ישראל" appropriate for the latter part of Rav Yochanan's statement? Are we "fortunate" when we don't obey Hashem and our suffering is worse than anyone else's? He answers that since the punishments are "abnormal" (למעלה מן הטבע, beyond what is natural) it is obvious that they are from Hashem. Just as a child finds comfort when he sees that it is his father, rather than a stranger, who is punishing him, so too Klal Yisrael finds comfort knowing that it is Hashem who is "holding the rod."

No one can deny that the torture, suffering and pain which we endured during the Holocaust was למעלה מן הטבע – unparalleled in the annals of civilized nations. Perhaps comfort can be found in the words of Rav Yehonasan Eibeshitz.

May we earn Hashem's speedy *Geulah*, which we so desperately need and long for.

What strategies can we use to strengthen our *emunah* daily?

It is the ability to internalize the message of "אשריכם ישראל" that distinguishes good from great people. The following story is a case in point.

Rabbi Elimelech and Ruthy Goldberg were newly married when they were blessed with what seemed to be a healthy little daughter. The first year of her life was quite normal, as she thrived and did everything that was expected. It was during the second year when her health became a major issue. She wasn't acting normally and the initial blood tests showed some irregularities. It was only after a few weeks that their beautiful daughter, Sora Basya, was diagnosed with leukemia. For the next few months the baby was in and out of the hospital, hooked up to various machines, monitoring her progress, in an effort to stabilize her health.

Despite the Goldbergs' noblest efforts, including the *tefillah* of the community and of many prominent individuals, the prognosis was not good. I was with Rabbi Goldberg in the Intensive Care Unit of UCLA Medical Center as Sora Basya's every heartbeat was being monitored on screen. The graph spiked each time the heart beat. It was at that moment that I learned how a *yerei Shamayim* faces tragedy. *Each* time the graph peaked Rabbi Goldberg uttered the words, *"Baruch Hashem, Baruch Hashem..."* Although he fully realized that his daughter's heart may cease to function at any moment, he drew inspiration knowing that she was in the Hands of a loving G-d.

Sora Basya's brief life came to an end on כ"א חשון, תשמ"ב. How appropriate it was that she returned her *neshamah* in the week of פרשת חיי שרה.

תהא נשמתה צרורה בצרור החיים

On Being Content

Twice each day there is a mitzvah to recite the Shema. The first *parshah*, which is contained in this week's *sedra*, commands us to love Hashem, "with all your heart (בכל לבבך), and with all your soul (ובכל נפשך), and with all your resources (ובכל מאדך)." According to Rabbi Samson Raphael Hirsch זצ"ל, "a love that is not prepared to make the sacrifice of even the smallest physical desires is a vain pretense."

The Gemara (*Brachos* 54a) learns from the words ובכל מאדך that the mitzvah of loving Hashem applies to every situation in life, whether it be good or bad. The Chafetz Chaim provides us with a perspective that can help us understand this mandate. Each individual is tested in life, so that his or her specific potential can be realized. Thus everyone's portion (חֵלֶק) in life has been "custom designed" to suit his *neshamah's* specifications. When a person can rejoice with his portion, he is considered rich (*Pirkei Avos* 4:1). He sees his or her circumstances as an opportunity to fulfill his personal mission, despite any hardships or challenges. This is then reason to express one's love for Hashem.

Blessings of intelligence, health or wealth are also customized tests designed to assess a person's level of humility and gratitude. Thus the Navi (*Yirmiyahu* 9:22) warns the wise person not to brag about his wisdom, nor the mighty person to speak of his own strength (health) or the wealthy person to talk about his own wealth. Why boast about one's tests; it's the results which count!!

Being content in life means internalizing this reality. Perhaps we could say that in the Shema we are directed to serve Hashem with these same three attributes:

· בכל לבבך – with all *your* intelligence (as we say in *davening*, וְתֵן בְּלִבֵּנוּ – לְהָבִין וּלְהַשְׂכִּיל – *put into our hearts the ability to understand*)

· ובכל נפשך – and with all *your* (degree of) health (which maintains your soul)

· ובכל מאדך – and with all *your* wealth.

None of these gifts are distributed equally. Our "job" is to be content with *our* lot as we properly direct them in His service.

What attitude do *you* need to reinforce to become more content?

It was during the 1991 Persian-Gulf War that every Jewish heart and mind was focused on Eretz Yisrael. Would Iraq succeed in its sinister plan to launch missiles toward the Holy Land in an attempt to kill innocent Jewish souls? We in school were reminding our students that *tefillah* is that all-powerful vehicle which we need to employ to help our brothers and sisters in Israel. One high school student came to me innocently, questioning my approach. She could not understand what benefit *her tefillah* could possibly have, since there were far more righteous people than she who were *davening*. If Hashem would not heed their *tefillos* why should He heed her prayers?

I tried to give her an answer which I thought was accurate and which she could "digest." I explained that *tefillah* is a mitzvah which originates in the heart and ends on one's lips. As such, Hashem does not simply hear the words but He "assesses" each heart – the source of the *tefillah*. Since each person was given a distinct portion in life, each person's *tefillah* is unique. No one else in the whole world lives in the same setting, in the same family, has the same personality traits with the same strengths or challenges. Sincere *tefillah* is a product of one's total situation and thus each and every person's *davening* is distinctive. Each *tefillah* has its own "ingredients" and its own special power.

The young lady seemed to be satisfied, although I can only speculate if she translated this into "action."

Bemoan your ill fate
with great caution.

**DARE YOU FORGET ALL
YOUR GOOD FORTUNE.**

סוֹמֵךְ ה' לְכָל הַנֹּפְלִים וְזוֹקֵף לְכָל הַכְּפוּפִים (תהלים קמה, יד)

Hashem's Hidden Hand

In the beginning of the *sedra*, Bnei Yisrael are encouraged to enter Eretz Canaan with confidence, assuming that they have observed the mitzvos. Hashem assures them that they will enjoy personal *brachah*, in addition to an overwhelming victory against the nations that occupy Eretz Yisrael. And just as He defeated the Egyptians with "wonders and miracles," so too will He vanquish the multitude of people before you; the Jewish people need not fear. The Torah explains that Hashem will send the צרעה – the hornet-swarm – to rout the enemy, "for Hashem, your G-d, is among you; a *great* and *awesome* G-d." What is the significance behind the צרעה, and the reference here to a "great and awesome G-d"?

Rabbeinu Bacheye explains that Hashem runs the world through two types of miracles. There are those which are covert or hidden (נסים נסתרים) and there are those which are overt or obvious (נסים מפורסמים). The introductory *pesukim* of our *parshah* tell us of Hashem's "wonders and miracles," the open miracles that Hashem employed to defeat the Mitzriyim. Now Hashem informs His people that there is also another "unit in His cavalry" which He plans to call into action: הצרעה. The hornet-swarm is part of His covert miracles, as they are a natural phenomenon. Just as rain is part of nature and is used to reward or punish people, so too the hornet will be used against the enemy. The reference to Hashem as גדול ונורא – *great and awesome*, continues Rabbeinu Bacheye, is referring to the role Hashem plays in both types of miracles: גדול in His covert miracles, and נורא in His overt miracles.

Today Hashem operates primarily through נסים נסתרים, which we call *hashgachah pratis* – personal supervision. Rav Shimon Schwab זצ"ל writes in his commentary on the siddur that, "Each day we thank Hashem, ועל נסיך שבכל יום עמנו – *for Your miracles which are with us each day*. This refers to the hidden miracles with which our lives are filled, that we may not even be aware of since אין בעל הנס מכיר בנסו – the recipient of a miracle does not realize his miracle. A person could contract a major illness, which, were it seen by a doctor would be diagnosed as such, but then it miraculously passes and he is never aware of it and none the worse for it" (page 515).

Our life-long obligation is to try to recognize Hashem's Hidden Hand in all of its manifestations.

Why is it so easy not to see the Hand of Hashem?

Our family's move from New York to Los Angeles in 1978 seemed to be the right thing to do. I was looking to expand my experience in *chinuch* so I interviewed in L.A. and after some negotiations I accepted an administrative position there. Some of our friends could not believe that we would move to the West Coast but we were a young couple with five children and the opportunity seemed good. To be on the safe side, I made a stipulation with my new employer that, if this new employment did not succeed, he would cover the cost of the return plane tickets.

The first few months on the job went fairly well, with only minor complications. As time progressed, however, there were more concerns, and although all parties wanted it to work, it did not seem promising. I was in contact with a colleague of mine in New York, Rabbi Yoel Kramer, asking him for guidance on how best to negotiate this difficult situation.

The academic year was three-quarters over and, preferring to remain on the West Coast, I hesitantly decided to continue my position for the next year. One day I received a most welcomed phone call from Rav Moshe Meiselman, former *rosh yeshivah* of YULA. He asked me if I would consider the position of principal of a new high school which they were planning to open in September. After several meetings and after being released from my previous commitment, I gladly accepted this new position.

I wondered, though, how YULA knew that I was looking to switch positions. I found out that one of the *beis midrash rabbeim* had called his mentor on the East Coast, who was none other than Rabbi Yoel Kramer. He asked him if he knew of an appropriate candidate in New York to fill this new position. Rabbi Kramer, knowing my situation, told him that there was a candidate right in L.A. who would love a change and he gave him my name.

Until today I marvel at the *hashgachah pratis* which enabled me to leave a difficult position for a new one which lasted for fifteen years, *baruch Hashem*.

The Hand of Hashem is NOT always easy to see; LOOK CAREFULLY TO UNCOVER HIS MAJESTY

מודים אנחנו לך... ועל נסיך שבכל יום עמנו (מתוך הסידור)

Read – What You See!

The opening *pesukim* of this week's *sedra* instruct Bnei Yisrael to see (ראה) that Hashem is placing before them a blessing and a curse. The *brachah* will be realized when Hashem's mitzvos are followed and a *klalah* (curse) will result if the commandments are not obeyed. According to Ramban (as opposed to Rashi) this is a general statement which is not related to the blessings and curses given on *Har Gerizim* and *Har Eival* (later in פרק כ"ז).

There are two points which beg clarification: 1) The *pesukim* do not explain which blessings and curses are being referred to. 2) The wording of the first *pasuk* starts in the singular form (ראה – see) and continues in the plural form (לפניכם – before you [many]). Rav Moshe Feinstein זצ"ל has a novel interpretation of these *pesukim* which illuminates their meaning. He says that the same item which may be a source of happiness for one person, can be a source of aggravation for another. A car, for example, may be viewed, from the perspective of a person immersed in Torah and mitzvos, as a tremendous blessing. For the non-thinking Jew, however, it can be a source of selfish, arrogant pride and cause for indignation toward his neighbor whose car may be bigger or better. This is true of one's home, family or any other asset which a person normally benefits from.

Accordingly, the Torah is stating that the gifts that are placed before mankind (לפניכם) may be a blessing or a curse, depending on each individual's perspective (ראה). This explains the switch from singular to plural. And what our perception is, depends on our commitment to Hashem's mitzvos. The Torah is thus not coming to teach us *which* items are a blessing or a curse, but rather *how* to make sure that each individual sees (לשון יחיד) his blessings as such. The more our thinking is "powered" by Torah, the more we will be able to appreciate and discern Hashem's gifts.

Why is it so easy to "misread" what we see?

Appreciating all the *brachos* which we enjoy depends on our outlook on life and our ability to see the whole picture. The following story is a case in point.

It was a beautiful Sunday afternoon in Los Angeles and our family decided to make a barbeque on the front porch. I retrieved our old grill, threw coals into it and placed it flush upon the decorative ceramic tile which covered our broad concrete wall around the porch. I felt that the situation was safe, since there were no combustible or flammable materials visible. After firing up the coals, we cooked hot dogs and burgers and concluded a delicious meal. After everyone left, I doused the coals with plenty of water to make sure that the fire was totally extinguished. I left the scene but I was called back shortly afterward by my wife. There was smoke rising from the concrete walls! I assumed that it was simply excess heat and I sprayed some cold water on it from our water hose. This did not help and the concrete wall continued to emit smoke. I was totally puzzled and I reluctantly bowed to my wife's cries to call 911. On the phone, I innocently asked them not to turn on their sirens, so as not to draw too much attention.

Within minutes the fire engines came blazing down our street, with lights and sirens roaring. The firefighters jumped off their trucks and in seconds they assessed the situation. They grasped the ceramic tile with their bare hands and yanked it off. Inside the concrete wall was a wooden frame which was raging with fire. They quickly extinguished the flames and explained to me this strange phenomenon. The ceramic tile apparently conducted the extreme heat of the grill and ignited the wood frame, hidden within the concrete wall. Had they arrived minutes later the whole house would have gone up in flames.

I made a serious error in judgment since I did not see the full picture. Being able to assess accurately all that we have, means seeing all our wealth with the accompanying Invisible Hand.

Wealth is not hidden nor in disguise; ALL YOU NEED IS TO OPEN YOUR EYES.

-Sheva Kipper

ראה אנכי נתן לפניכם היום ברכה וקללה (יא, כו)

Faith in Our Chachamim

Rambam teaches us that when the Beis Hamikdash stood, the Great Sanhedrin (בית דין הגדול) in Yerushalayim was the final arbiter between differing opinions regarding the interpretation of the Written Torah. This is derived from the *pasuk* in our *sedra* which states, *You shall not deviate from the word that they will tell you* (17:11). Rashi says that this applies even if they say that "the right is left and the left is right."

The *Sefer Hachinuch* explains that this mitzvah includes the obligation to listen to our earlier sages and to the Torah scholars in *our* generation. He advances his view that the prohibition of לא תסור (not to deviate) applies even when you *know* that their ruling is incorrect; even if they say that the "right is left." He explains that the detriment of undermining the authority of the *chachamim* is far greater than committing an occasional mistake. He writes, "Better to tolerate one error and have everyone under their beneficent rule, than each person doing as he pleases."

With this approach the *Sefer Hachinuch* explains the Gemara (*Bava Metzia* 59b) in which Rabi Eliezer and the *chachamim* argue whether a particular type of oven is susceptible to *tumah* (impurity). Rabi Eliezer performed miracles to support his opinion that it is not susceptible. He even summoned a *Bas Kol* (Heavenly Voice) to affirm his position. Despite this, his opinion was rejected since לא בשמים היא – *It (Torah) is not in Heaven*. Halachah is subject to the guidelines given by Hashem to Moshe at Har Sinai, which dictates to follow the majority opinion; to that of the *chachamim*. The Gemara concludes that, after this ruling, Eliyahu Hanavi reported that Hashem was "laughing" and saying, "נִצְחוּנִי בָּנַי – *My children have prevailed over Me*." The *Sefer Hachinuch* explains that although Rabi Eliezer was ultimately correct, Hashem was happy that his opinion was not followed. Hashem rejoiced knowing that His people surrendered their understanding to the Divine process of halachah. Conforming to His will was more important than doing what was empirically true.

> **Why is it significant that Jewish Law is called "Halachah"?**

Rabbi Zalman Ury זצ"ל was the senior consultant for Orthodox schools in Los Angeles for many decades. He was a *talmid* of Rav Aharon Kotler זצ"ל in Kletzk, and came to L.A. after the war. He was beloved by all of the members of the community and led the Yeshivah Principals Council with integrity, understanding and great vision. Every year he would visit his children in Eretz Yisrael and return to L.A. inspired through the *kedushas Ha'Aretz*. His ultimate dream was to retire and settle in Eretz Yisrael.

In the mid 1980s Rabbi Ury felt that the time had come to realize his dream. A warm farewell party was hosted for Rabbi and Mrs. Ury and they left for their new home in Israel.

After their move, an unbelievable thing happened. Rabbi and Mrs. Ury returned to L.A., to the happy surprise of everyone. No one really knew what actually transpired and Rabbi Ury once again resumed his position, part time. To the members of the Yeshivah Principals Council he confided and shared the following story. Upon coming to Eretz Yisrael he visited the *gadol hador*, Rabbi Eliezer Shach זצ"ל, whom he knew from Europe. Rav Shach asked him what he was doing in Eretz Yisrael and Rabbi Ury responded that he had come to settle there. Rav Shach told him that he should return to L.A. since it was there that Klal Yisrael needed him the most. Rav Shach was aging and Rabbi Ury thought that perhaps the *gadol hador* did not fully understand the situation. Rabbi Ury waited a few weeks and returned to Rav Shach. Again the exact conversation ensued with the same directive. Rabbi Ury then forfeited his life's dream to settle in Eretz Yisrael and returned to L.A., following the advice of the *gadol hador*.

Rabbi Ury was *niftar* in 2002 and was laid to rest on Har Hamenuchos in the Land that he longed to live.

תהא נפשו צרורה בצרור החיים

Following our chachamim is a Torah priority;

BETTER THAT WE ERR, THAN TO UNDERMINE THEIR AUTHORITY.

לֹא תָסוּר מִן הַדָּבָר אֲשֶׁר יַגִּידוּ לְךָ יָמִין וּשְׂמֹאל (יז, יא)

פרשת כי תצא
Trusting in Hashem

Our *sedra* concludes with the mitzvah of remembering what Amalek did to us as we left Mitzrayim. Unprovoked, they launched a sneak attack against a nation for whom Hashem had performed outright miracles. By doing so they displayed hatred, not only toward the Jewish people but also toward their G-d.

Directly preceding these *pesukim* the Torah admonishes Klal Yisrael to distance themselves from dishonesty. For example, not only may a Jew not use false weights and measures when buying or selling goods, he may not even own them.

Rashi explains that the mitzvah of remembering Amalek is placed right after we are cautioned to be honest since dishonest behavior will bring "the roar of the enemy" (גרוי האויב) upon us. But why should this particular *aveirah* lead to Amalek? Rav Moshe Feinstein זצ"ל explains that deceptive behavior reflects a lack of *bitachon* (trust) in Hashem's ability to provide for one's needs. This same denial of the power of Hashem was found in Amalek, as they arrogantly pounced upon the Jewish "weak and exhausted." Thus, people who swindle and whose actions reflect denial of Hashem, are punished by those who repudiated Hashem's power.

Rav Moshe explains that this approach is consistent with the Torah's narration of Amalek's attack in *Parshas Beshalach* (פרק י"ז). There the story is preceded with the account of Refidim, where Moshe Rabbeinu was forced to bring forth water from a rock. Bnei Yisrael challenged Hashem's ability to support them in the wilderness by asking, "Is Hashem among us or not?" Rashi explains that Amalek's attack directly follows this event as a response to demonstrate Hashem's presence. Although Rashi presents another explanation there for its juxtaposition, it is based upon the same principle: Klal Yisrael will "force Hashem's Hand" when they doubt His ability to care for them, directly or indirectly, individually or collectively.

What tips would you give your friend to remember Hashem's ever-presence?

Periodically, small "coincidences" occur in one's life which serve to remind us that Hashem is watching.

The first such event took place in our home in Los Angeles in 1986. Rav Moshe Feinstein had just been *niftar* and Yidden throughout the world were thrown into mourning for this undisputed *gadol hador*. *Hespedim* were delivered in every Jewish metropolis. Our entire family went to one such gathering on Motza'ei Shabbos, where Rav Moshe's humility and greatness were touted. After two hours of eulogies we came home and sat around our living room, reviewing the highlights of all the speeches. At one point I said that I really couldn't believe that at the moment that Rav Moshe died, the light by the seat in his yeshivah went out. Just as I finished my sentence, all the lights in our living room went out. A frightening hush descended on our family, as I sheepishly retracted my statement. (It seems that "coincidentally" the Shabbos clock had not been reset.)

Another incident occurred a few years ago in Baltimore on Erev Rosh Hashanah. My wife had finished all her food shopping, which included about half a dozen apples, to dip into the honey. One of our married sons came over and asked if we had any apples to spare so that he could fulfill this *minhag* in the evening. Although we really had no extras, she gave him all the apples. My wife preferred to make a second trip rather than to inconvenience this child (who had children with special needs at home). About five minutes later, there was a knock on the door. Our next-door neighbor had gone apple picking and wanted to share his "harvest." He presented us with a bag in which there were just about half a dozen apples. You can just imagine the depth of meaning that was carried in that bag.

Don't tell Hashem how big your problems are,

TELL YOUR PROBLEMS HOW BIG HASHEM IS.

(AUTHOR UNKNOWN)

בטח אל ה' בכל לבך ואל בינתך על תשען (משלי ג, ה)

Gratitude

This week's *parshah* begins with the mitzvah of *bikurim* – bringing one's first fruits (of the Seven Species) up to Yerushalayim to the *kohen* in the Beis Hamikdash. After waiting patiently and working hard on his field in Eretz Yisrael, the farmer is now ready to enjoy the fruits of his labor. But he must first express his appreciation to Hashem. Rashi comments, שאינך כפוי טובה – the purpose of this declaration is to demonstrate that he is not ungrateful. The Torah states that he must recognize "that Hashem took us out of Egypt with a strong hand…and He brought us to this place." The farmer thus recalls the previous difficulties and earlier challenges that his people endured, before he could benefit from the bounty of the land.

Rabbeinu Bacheye gleans from this a lesson for life: a person, having now triumphed, must remember the valley of despair that he or his ancestors may have gone through, in order for him to have reached his state of success.

Too often we think that the way it is now, is the way it always was. But that's usually not the case. Take Baltimore, for example. Our predecessors had to work hard to deepen religious commitment and practice so that we now have a plethora of shuls and schools in our town.

What "view" are you now enjoying and to whom should you direct your gratitude?

My father-in-law, Rabbi Eliyahu Meir Weinberger זצ"ל, was a second and third grade *rebbi* in Toras Emes Kaminetz in Brooklyn, New York for over forty-five years.

He often recalled the difficult days of his youth in Vienna, Austria, and how Hashem miraculously saved him from the hands of the Nazis ימ"ש. He told us about the ruthlessness of the Nazis ימ"ש (even pre-WWII) and how the Jews were humiliated to scrub the streets on their hands and knees. They ordered the Jews to erase slogans of hate, which the Nazis themselves wrote, in order to frame the Jews. Yidden would be grabbed off the street and forced into a car, never to be seen again. They were forced to wear signs declaring "*Ich bin a schwein*" (I am a pig). He never forgot the day of his bar mitzvah in 1938, at which time he was directed not to go to the Schiff Shul since it was too dangerous. His bar mitzvah was held in the home of the *rav*, with only his mother present since his father had died earlier. Little Eliyahu Meir's life was spared through the "Kindertransport" (children's train) from Vienna to Cardiff, England, in 1938. This was arranged by Mr. Julius Steinfeld ז"ל and Rabbi Solomon Schonfeld ז"ל and his gratitude toward these "giants" who saved his life never ceased.

On my father-in-law's seventy-sixth birthday, he made mention of the many students to whom he had taught Torah and the many smiles that he had brought to their faces. He said that since Hashem spared his life he felt that he had to "earn his keep"! He did not want to be ungrateful and he therefore dedicated his life to teaching Hashem's Torah to His children.

When you enjoy the view from the top, APPRECIATE THOSE WHO PREPARED THAT SPOT.

ארמי אובד אבי... ויבאנו על המקום הזה (כו, ה-ט)

פרשת נצבים
Standing Together

The entire Jewish people are gathered together, poised to enter Eretz Yisrael, on the last day of Moshe Rabbeinu's life. They have come to accept the obligations that Hashem's chosen people, a Torah nation, must carry. The question that begs to be asked is why this was necessary again. They had already affirmed their allegiance to Hashem at Har Sinai when they received the Torah!

Rabbeinu Bacheye presents one answer by saying that their previous acceptance was rendered void as soon as they served the Golden Calf. A second answer given is that a new acceptance was necessary as they were about to enter Eretz Yisrael, where life would be different than it was in the *Midbar*. A life of open miracles would be replaced with a more natural way of living. Rashi and others explain that this new acceptance merely expanded on their former commitment and added the quality of *achrayus* (responsibility for one another), which would take effect as soon as they entered the Holy Land.

Whatever the reason for this reaffirmation, it is happening right after Hashem warned them of the severe consequences (in *Parshas Ki Savo*) that the Jewish people would bring upon themselves if they failed to follow the Torah. The Midrash, quoted by Rashi, uses this juxtaposition to explain why the opening words of our *sedra* are, *You stand (Nitzavim) today..."* Moshe is reassuring and comforting his people by saying that despite the ninety-eight curses mentioned previously, you continue to exist as a people; you are standing upright, firm, purposeful (not just "*Omdim*," a softer word for "standing"). You needn't fear that the Jewish nation will be obliterated even if they do sin.

The Midrash reinforces this message by focusing on the third word of the opening *pasuk*, "today." Just as the Jewish day begins with night and is followed by day, so too, our darkness (the difficult times) will be followed by light. We are eternally optimistic, despite the dark and painful *galus* we are experiencing. We trust implicitly in Hashem and His Torah and in the words of His Navi (*Michah* 7:8), *When I fall, I shall arise. When I sit in darkness, Hashem is a light to me!*

> **What is the significance of the Jewish people standing together?**

If there was ever a colossal *kiddush Hashem* of Jews standing together, shoulder-to-shoulder, in modern times, it took place on Wednesday evening, August 1, 2012, the 13th of Av, 5772. This is when 92,000(!!) Yidden came together to celebrate the Twelfth Siyum HaShas of Daf Yomi in the MetLife Stadium in East Rutherford, New Jersey. People representing the entire spectrum of the Orthodox community *davened* together, learned together, listened together and danced together. There was a feeling of spiritual euphoria which swept through the stadium, proclaiming through our presence that there is no other nation like Yisrael.

In his opening remarks, the Master of Ceremonies noted that on this very day in 1936, Hitler ימ"ש opened the Olympic games in Berlin, Germany, in a similar setting. In a stadium filled with tens of thousands of people, this ruthless leader tried to show off the might of his nation as he hid his sinister plot to destroy the Jewish people. Yet seventy-six years later we stood together celebrating the eternity of Hashem and His Torah, as our enemies have fallen by the wayside. Our enemies could not extinguish the eternal spark of the Torah, and the embers from the ashes of the Holocaust have been rekindled to create a blaze which knows no bounds.

Rav Yisroel Meir Lau, Chief Rabbi of Tel Aviv and former Chief Rabbi of Israel, pointed out that the *Shir Shel Yom* of Wednesday is *perek* 94 in Tehillim, which describes Hashem as a "G-d of vengeance" (*Kel Nekamos*). He then went on to explain that the outpouring of Jews present in this arena tonight is the realization of the next words of this *pasuk*: *Kel nekamos hofia* – "G-d of vengeance appear!" Tonight was the ultimate revenge against those prophets of Jewish doom. Rabbi Lau expressed in those few words what everyone present felt. An indescribable *kavod Shamayim* was taking place and we were experiencing a historic moment. No wonder the day-long rain showers ceased just as the program began. This was to be a moment like no other.

KLAL YISRAEL IS HERE FOREVER;
let us all stand together.

אתם נצבים היום כולכם (כט, ט)

Our Yellow Light

Our *sedra* discusses the mitzvah of *Hakhel*, the gathering of the entire Klal Yisrael to hear the king read from the Torah in the Beis Hamikdash. This event coincided with the first day of Chol Hamoed Sukkos as Bnei Yisrael were being *oleh regel*, going up to Yerushalayim for Yom Tov. This event was relatively rare since it only occurred once in seven years, right after the termination of the *shemittah* year.

What purpose did this mitzvah serve? The Torah itself says, *So that they will hear and so that they will learn and they shall fear Hashem* (31:12). The *Sefer Hachinuch* elaborates and explains that Torah is that which sets us apart from all other people and through it we can merit eternal pleasure. This enormous, monumental gathering of men, women and children assembling to hear the Torah, drives home this point and motivates our people to learn and to love Torah.

The question which one can ask, however, is why Hashem, in His infinite wisdom, specifically placed this mitzvah following the *shemittah* year. The *Meshech Chachmah* suggests that *Hakhel* facilitates the transition from a year immersed in Torah learning to a return to routine labor. During the Sabbatical year people were busy learning since they were forbidden to work on their field, and they had few distractions. Torah inspires a person to grow spiritually and not to be greedy, jealous or lustful. Now that the *shemittah* year is over he needs a boost and a dramatic reminder not to run "headlong" back to work. With the mitzvah of *Hakhel*, Hashem is emphasizing the need to pause and reflect on our new vulnerability when we are no longer totally immersed in Torah.

The mitzvah of *Hakhel* serves as a figurative "yellow light" to slow down and to "proceed with caution" as one re-enters society. Torah keeps us on track, making sure that our values, priorities and sensitivities are correct. Without it we may adopt values and practices that are foreign to true Jewish living.

How can the low standards of society affect us?

Living in a democratic country, as we do in America, is a genuine blessing. We live in an open society free to practice our religion as we please, without fear of persecution. What wouldn't our grandparents and great-grandparents have given to live their Yiddishkeit as we do? Yet we pay a price living without laws or walls to separate us from the non-Jewish world. Their values, dress and speech slowly creep into our lives, as the sensitivities toward our Torah's standards become diluted.

In the late 1980s I was the head counselor in Camp Mesorah, an overnight camp in the San Bernardino mountains, just east of Los Angeles. We serviced primarily the L.A. yeshivah community in this beautiful campsite. In order to inject the camp with a *ruach haTorah* we "imported" some *beis midrash bachurim* from the East Coast, with their *rosh yeshivah*. The boys came up several days before the campers in order to orient themselves with the staff and with the entire setting. I took advantage of the situation and addressed the *bachurim* in the presence of their *rosh yeshivah*. I wanted to "charge them" with the responsibility to interact positively with the campers, so that their presence would be an asset to the camp. I began my talk and said to the group: "You have a great opportunity, guys, to be exemplary role models for our campers." At this point, the *rosh yeshivah* politely stood up and addressed me by saying, "Rabbi Hexter, these are *not* 'guys' – they're *bachurim*." I smiled, nodded in agreement and continued my *shmuess*.

I learned a great lesson. I realized how much my speech was affected by the outside environment. I also learned how important it is to address people, even those who are younger than you, with respect.

The Gemara teaches us to always use *lashon nekiyah*, clean and refined language. Speech is that which distinguishes man from animal and elevates us from the common folk around us. How careful we must be to make sure that our mouths are powered by the Torah's guidelines and not by society's mores.

Our Torah shines
so very bright.

DON'T LET SOCIETY
DIM ITS LIGHT.

כי באור פניך נתת לנו, ה' אלקנו, תורת חיים ואהבת חסד
(מתוך הסידור)

Scaling the Skies

הצור תמים פעלו כי כל דרכיו משפט א-ל אמונה ואין עול צדיק וישר הוא
(לב, ד)

Hashem's work is perfect for all His paths are just, He is a G-d of faith without sin, righteous and fair is He.

Here the Torah sums up the Jewish attitude toward suffering. It is referred to as *tziduk hadin*, accepting (or righting) Hashem's judgment. Hashem is perfect, yet our perception of what may seem bad is flawed due to our inability to comprehend His ways. Although an episode may be bitter, it is never bad. Our limited understanding of the *neshamah* (soul) precludes us from knowing its particular source, specific challenges, and its ultimate mission. Our years on earth expose us only to a small part of the puzzle called life. What we do know is that Hashem is a compassionate and loving Father Who brought us into this world and Who will be with us forever.

In *Parshas Beshalach* (15:26), Hashem refers to Himself as our Doctor. The Malbim explains that just as a doctor may need to impose pain on a patient in order to remedy a situation, so too, Hashem. He may need to bring pain onto His children, *chas v'shalom*, not for punitive, but rather for therapeutic, purposes. That's why our *chachamim* instruct us to live constantly by the maxim: כל מה דעביד רחמנא לטב עביד – *All that Hashem does is for the best.*

What difficulties have you been faced with and how did you face the challenge?

Let me share with you a short, personal incident with a profound message.

The snow was coming down heavily as I sat by my window seat ready to take off for Detroit, Michigan. I hadn't seen my ailing uncle for quite a while, and I was anxious to get there safely. Given the inclement weather, I was jittery, especially since many other flights had been canceled that day. Due to the heavy fog and falling snow, the only thing I could see was the ground crew busily plowing, trying to clear the tarmac. Slowly, the plane taxied to be "de-iced," after which it gracefully took off, almost magically leaving behind the storm. As the plane pierced the clouds, the bright sun beamed through my tiny window, warming my face and calming my nerves. I eagerly opened my Tehillim to where I was up to. To my astonishment the *pasuk* read:

ענן וערפל סביביו, צדק ומשפט מכון כסאו (צז, ב)

Clouds and heavy fog surround Him, righteousness and justice are the foundation of His seat.

What was Hashem telling me? Could it be that this experience was a metaphor for life itself? The message that I heard was that Hashem is always fair and kind, just like the sun is always shining. We need, however, to be able to lift ourselves above our "clouds" – our fears and idiosyncrasies.

At times we must "de-ice" – to shed our preconceived notions and attitudes, to scale the skies so that we can rise above the moment to appreciate His goodness. When we place our problems into the proper perspective and filter them through the prism of Torah, they dwarf and melt from rays of hope.

Hashem is our Doctor, some medicine is sour;

REMEMBER THAT IN A DIFFICULT HOUR.

כל המחלה אשר שמתי במצרים לא אשים עליך
כי אני ה' רפאך (שמות טו, כו)

It's All Good

The Torah describes the demise of Moshe Rabbeinu in this last *sedra*: *So Moshe, servant of Hashem, died there in the land of Moav... He buried him in the valley* (34:6-7). The Gemara (*Sotah* 14a) comments that just as the Torah begins with Hashem performing an act of *chessed*, it concludes with one as well. Just as in *Parshas Bereishis* Hashem makes garments of skins for Adam and his wife (3:21), the Torah concludes with the act of *chessed* of Moshe's burial. The Ksav Sofer is somewhat perplexed with this statement. Why is the Gemara simply stating the obvious? Furthermore, according to another opinion, it wasn't Hashem who buried Moshe, but rather Moshe who buried himself. How is this an example of *chessed*?

The Ksav Sofer answers and elucidates our understanding of the Gemara. By calling the burying of Moshe Rabbeinu an act of *chessed*, the Gemara is saying that it was good, albeit bitter and sad. "All that Hashem does is good." Sometimes it is sweet, as when Hashem made clothing for Adam and Chava, and sometimes it is bitter, as when Moshe died and was buried.

But how can dying be called good when it is tragic? The Jewish outlook on life recognizes two parts; one of the body in this world, and one of the soul in the World-to-Come. A person may suffer *R"l*, or one's life may be cut short in this world, so that he can earn the ultimate reward in Gan Eden (Paradise). The Ksav Sofer further explains that Moshe was punished in this world for his sin by *Mei Merivah* (see *Bamidbar* 20:12) and he therefore died before he could lead Bnei Yisrael into the Promised Land. Moshe paid his debt, so to speak, in this world, so that he could receive his true reward in *Olam Haba*. This is the point that the Gemara is making. The sweet *chessed* Hashem performed in *Bereishis* is compared to the bitter *chessed* that Moshe received by being buried on the other side of the Jordan before entering Eretz Yisrael.

I am reminded of the story that the newspapers reported when Rav Moshe Feinstein was *niftar* in 1986. Thousands of people came to mourn his loss in the Lower East Side of New York. One policeman who observed all the crying and moaning of the masses asked one of the participants: "Why is everyone crying? He lived a long and productive life." The participant responded: "We are not crying for the deceased; his life was long and he is receiving the ultimate reward in Paradise. We are crying for ourselves. We will sorely miss him." Both were good, although one was sweet and the other was bitter.

Why is it so difficult to deal with the "thorns" in life?

The dining hall of Yeshiva Chemdas Levovos* was packed with friends and family. They were there to participate in the *seudas mitzvah* of the *bris* of Shlomo Katzer. What was so unusual about this event was that little Shlomo was about to turn four years old. Shlomo was born prematurely, which compounded existing complications. He immediately required emergency surgery to separate the food pipe from the wind pipe, which were abnormally connected. Throughout the first three years of his life, the medical problems which challenged his breathing, digestion and neurological function impeded his healthy, normal development. This precluded the possibility of an early *bris*. Shlomo frequently spent time in the hospital for days or weeks and sometimes for months. One would expect that the physical and emotional strain on a family in such a hectic situation would cause total chaos. Incredibly, the parents, Lena and Dovid, never lost focus. Their positive, upbeat, optimistic mood, filled with *tefillah* and *bitachon*, carried the family. The incredible support of the Jewish community was always there for them, helping to maintain a sense of relative normalcy in the home.

During the *seudah*, a slide show was shown tracing Shlomo's miraculous growth, despite all odds. For example, in his early years, Shlomo had a dangerous inflammation of his small intestines which required exploratory surgery. The surgeon on duty refused to do the operation, fearing that Shlomo's small body would be unable to survive such trauma. However, a dedicated NICU nurse, seeing that Shlomo's life was in the balance, connected with the original surgeon, who interrupted his vacation to come and successfully perform the surgery. This saved Shlomo's life.

At a later point in Shlomo's development, he failed to thrive, and the team of neonatologists and GI specialists did not understand why. Fast forward a few months. Shlomo is rushed to the hospital with a life-threatening blood infection from his I.V. line, due to a bacteria which is normally found in the stomach. To treat that infection, the doctors put him on a strong antibiotic, after which Shlomo amazingly began to gain weight. It seems that Shlomo had a bacterial infection in his stomach which had been preventing him from gaining weight. Once he received the medication for his line infection, it "happened" to clear the intestinal infection as well. What was a scary, life-threatening incident, turned out to be a *yeshuah*. How could one not see *hashgachas Hashem*? Shlomo's condition, including epileptic seizures, only began to stabilize after his third birthday. The loving Hand of Hashem guided the Katzers every step of the way, including finding him an exclusive daycare therapeutic center, provided through the Childrens' Hospital.

At this *seudas mitzvah*, Dovid spoke about challenges that people go through in general. Through these *nisyonos* people have an opportunity to actualize hidden potential that they never realized they had. This certainly was the case with Shlomo and his family. The *chessed* of Hashem may be packaged with the fragrance of roses or at times accompanied with the sting of thorns. It's all *chasdei Hashem*!

*All names have been changed

Both roses
and thorns
ARE GIFTS
FROM HASHEM.

כל דעביד רחמנא לטב ביה (ברכות ס:)

Passing Life's Tests

קח נא את בנך... והעלהו שם לעולה (בראשית כב, ב)

(Hashem says to Avraham) "Please take your son... (Yitzchak) and bring him up there as an offering."

We read this *parshah* on the second day of Rosh Hashanah to draw upon the *rachamim* (mercy) that Hashem demonstrated toward Avraham and to Yitzchak. Hashem saw that Avraham was prepared to sacrifice his most beloved son, Yitzchak, and to surrender his will to the will of Hashem. Avraham had passed the test – the greatest test with which he could have been confronted.

Why does Hashem need to test people? Doesn't He know whether or not a person will pass? Ramban answers that through a test a human being actualizes the potential that rests dormant within him. By demonstrating those strengths he earns *zechuyos* (merits) which otherwise he could not access. Ramban writes that when one passes a test, he becomes worthy of receiving merit not only for a good heart but also for a good act. He continues to write:

כל הנסיונות שבתורה לטובת המנוסה... – *All the tests in the Torah are for the benefit of the one who is being tested.*

Every day each person is tested in one way or another:

· Should this be said or would it be better that it remain unsaid?

· Should I look or should I look away?

· Should I buy this outfit or should it remain on the rack?

During this time of the year, Hashem eagerly waits to see a change as we commit ourselves to improve our record of passing our daily tests.

What strategies could *you* employ to pass your daily tests?

In 1980, world Jewry focused its attention on the untenable plight of Yosef Mendelevich, a Russian Refusenik jailed behind the Iron Curtain. Ten years earlier, he was accused of trying to hijack a plane to Israel in a scheme to dramatize the longings of Jews to leave the Soviet Empire. Throughout Mendelevich's incarceration he remained committed to *shemiras hamitzvos* even at the cost of brutal beatings.

At YULA in Los Angeles, we orchestrated a school-wide letter-writing campaign directed at politicians to pressure the Communist government to free Yosef Mendelevich. In 1981, after eleven years of imprisonment, he was released to finally realize his dream of moving to Eretz Yisrael.

We were deliriously happy as we felt that we played a small role in his release. The administration of the school decided to fly him to Los Angeles so that the students could hear firsthand about his experiences during his imprisonment.

At the assembly, Yosef Mendelevich recalled, in broken yet understandable English, his suffering in jail. He spoke of a situation in which he smuggled a siddur to his cell and was beaten up for his "crime." On Chanukah, he engraved a menorah in his cell wall and tore fibers, which acted as wicks, from his prison uniform. This was detected, and once again, he was beaten up. He explained modestly how he was relentless in his drive to perform mitzvos, regardless of the consequences.

After his presentation a high school girl from the audience raised her hand and innocently asked, "If you knew you were going to be beaten up, why did you continue to perform mitzvos?" Yosef Mendelevich commented that he didn't understand the question. The girl repeated the question, "If you knew that you were going to be beaten up, why did you continue to perform mitzvos?" Again he responded, saying that he didn't understand the question. She again repeated the question. Bewildered, he now exclaimed in a strong and forceful Russian accent, "Can you tell a tree *not* to be a tree?"

We sat stunned in silence. Yosef Mendelevich actually felt that he had no choice other than to perform his duties as a Jew. To him this was *not* a test. Would a tree discontinue practicing photosynthesis under the threat of punishment? We realized then that Yosef Mendelevich's inability to understand the question was not due to our superior command of the English language but rather due to our inferior appreciation of what it means to be an *eved Hashem* (servant of Hashem).

If you are going
in the wrong
direction,
HASHEM
WELCOMES
U-TURNS.

ושבת עד ה' אלקיך (נצבים ל, ב)

סוכות

Temporary or Permanent?

Upon analyzing the mitzvah of sukkah, we find an enigma. On the one hand, the *s'chach* has to be temporary (ארעי) in nature. Additionally, the walls cannot be taller than 20 *amos* (about 40 feet) since the construction would then be permanent by design. On the other hand, the halachah states that for the duration of Sukkos, one should make the sukkah his *permanent* dwelling (תשבו כעין תדורו). Is the operative term "temporary" or "permanent"?

Rav Nison Alpert זצ"ל explains that this dichotomy reflects the reality of Jewish life. We live a transient life – a life in which our soul is passing through this world as a temporary resident. Thus our sukkah is built as a temporary dwelling. Nevertheless, the mitzvos, standards and values by which we live are permanent and unchangeable. Reflecting this outlook, the halachah dictates that we perform the mitzvah of sukkah in a permanent fashion.

This is diametrically opposed to the world around us, whose philosophy is just the reverse. Their values and morals are constantly changing, and they believe that the life of the soul terminates with the body.

The duality of the mitzvah of sukkah demonstrates to every Jew that although life may be a fleeting moment in eternity, our mitzvos are fixed and immutable.

> Which mitzvos do we take for granted today that were "challenged" in the past?

Little did my father ז"ל know of the religious challenges which would await him here upon his arrival from Germany on November 3, 1938. He was a young man of nineteen and having learned under Rabbi Dr. Joseph Breuer in the Yeshivah of Frankfurt, he was committed to keeping Shabbos even in the "New World." His first job lasted two weeks as a "punch press" operator, making corrugated boxes. At his next job, he pushed hand racks in the garment district of Manhattan. That came to an end, as well, when he told his boss that he wouldn't work on Shabbos. The boss told him, "If you don't come in on Saturday, don't come in on Monday." After this "routine" repeated itself again, my father became discouraged and sought advice from a rabbi. Unbeknownst to my father, this "rabbi" was active in the (Conservative) Jewish Theological Seminary and subsequently recommended a position of employment to my father. My father, wanting to be reassured, asked rhetorically, "There will be no problem of keeping Shabbos, of course!" The "rabbi" looked at him quizzically, stating, "Shabbos? In America? עשה שבתך חול – *Make your Shabbos mundane*." He conveniently shortened and misrepresented the Gemara's assertion that on Shabbos it is better to eat a simple weekday meal rather than an elaborate Shabbos feast while having to borrow money to pay for it. My father realized immediately that this "rabbi" was a fraud, for he knew that Shabbos was Shabbos – even in America.

A short time later he was hired by a chemical cloth company where he was able to work five days a week. He retained this job for twenty-five years. In a clear case of Divine remuneration for his *shemiras Shabbos*, he was exempted from service during the military draft in WWII. This, because he was helping the war effort by supplying the army with treated cloths with which soldiers could clean their gun barrels.

Shabbos transcends the changes of time and place and is that eternal prototype reflecting the permanence of our Torah and its mitzvos.

ALTHOUGH THE
LIFE WE LIVE IS
TRANSIENT,

*the Torah's mitzvos
and values are
permanent.*

כל מצות שישראל עושין בעולם הזה באות ומעידות אותם
לעולם הבא (עבודה זרה ד:)

Sensitivity

The Torah recounts how Moshe and the Bnei Yisrael sang the *shirah* upon witnessing the great Hand of Hashem after the Yam Suf split.

נחית בחסדך עם זו גאלת (שמות טו, יג) – *With Your kindness You guided this people that You redeemed.*

The Chafetz Chaim quotes the *Tanna Dvei Eliyahu* on this *pasuk*. He says that when Klal Yisrael were in Mitzrayim they came together to agree on a joint pact. They accepted upon themselves the understanding that each one of them would extend kindness to the other. What is the relationship between "Hashem guiding His people with kindness" and the *chessed* that Klal Yisrael did for each other? The Chafetz Chaim explains that the sensitivity and kindness that Yidden extend to each other in *Olam Hazeh* awakens Divine beneficence in *Olam Haba*. This is consistent with the Gemara that states that Hashem will deal with us in the same measure with which we treat each other.

במידה שאדם מודד בה מודדין לו (מגילה יב:)

With this idea, the Chafetz Chaim explains the *brachah* of בורא נפשות. In it we say that Hashem created life, וחסרונן – *and their lackings*. Hashem filled His world with a total need for interdependence. That which one person needs, the other person can supply. This applies not only to financial issues, but to emotional ones as well. If an individual lacks happiness, there may be a friend who can comfort him – filling that gap. And the more *chessed* we perform among each other, the more Hashem showers us with His kindness.

This Divine reciprocity is described vividly by Mrs. Freeda Bassman in her novel, entitled *Miracles*. This Holocaust survivor attributes Hashem's kindness to her, due to her sensitive and selfless behavior to her friends during the war. Similarly, Mrs. Pearl Benisch describes in her book on Sarah Scheniner, *Carry Me in Your Heart*, how, during the Holocaust, Bais Yaakov girls risked their lives to share their morsels of bread with their friends.

מי יתן תמורתם

When was it most challenging to be sensitive to the needs of your friend?

It was in the mid 1980s that I visited Eretz Yisrael with a group of students from Los Angeles. I wanted to use the opportunity to meet with Rav Shlomo Zalman Auerbach זצ"ל and ask him a question concerning *geirus* (conversion) that arose in our school. On the morning of my planned visit to Rav Shlomo Zalman, I received a phone call from my wife. She was very bothered that in one of the schools in L.A., a class of third graders would routinely write down (and maintain) the names of the sick people on the blackboard and say Tehillim for them. The students sadly realized that some of the names were young children, and if *chas v'shalom* a child did not survive, that child's name was erased. This upset my wife terribly as she felt it wasn't good *chinuch* for children to *daven* for others (who they could identify with) and then to see their names deleted. She wanted me to share her feelings with the *gadol hador*, for perhaps it would be better not to say Tehillim at all.

I *davened* Minchah with Rav Shlomo Zalman, after which I accompanied him and his son to their home. After Rav Shlomo Zalman settled down in his study I entered and he welcomed me with a big smile. He first asked me some questions about my origins and was happy to hear that I had been a *talmid* in his yeshivah, Yeshivas Kol Torah, many years earlier. When I told him that I wanted to ask him some *she'eilos*, he humbly replied that I didn't have to travel halfway around the world to ask him. Concerning the first question of *geirus*, he responded without much deliberation and clearly gave me his *psak*. I then presented the second situation, which he thought about extensively as he stroked his beard, thinking quietly. He then confidently said that it was crucial for the children to continue saying Tehillim since: הקב"ה שומע לתפילות של תינוקות של בית רבן – *Hashem listens to the tefillos of children.* However, he concluded that there was no need to have the names of the *cholim* on the board to begin with. The continued saying of Tehillim, however, was paramount since children's *tefillos* are so powerful.

The *gadol hador* was sensitive to the feelings of those young children who could possibly be affected if a child's name was casually deleted. How much more so do we need to be aware of the possible consequences of every word we utter and every action we take.

Sensitivity is that special sign which reads:

YOUR SITUATION IS REALLY MINE.

יהי כבוד חברך חביב עליך כשלך (אבות ב, טו)

כל ישראל ערבים זה בזה (שבועות לט.)